The Minor Prophets
Mighty Messengers of God

A Bible Study Workbook
By Matthew Allen

Published by
Spiritbuilding Publishers
9700 Ferry Road, Waynesville, Ohio 45068

THE MINOR PROPHETS
Mighty Messengers of God
By Matthew Allen

ISBN: 978–1955285–68–1

Spiritbuilding
PUBLISHERS

spiritbuilding.com

Acknowledgments

First written in 2006, this study on the Minor Prophets has gone far and wide. It was my first major attempt at an in-depth and comprehensive Bible study workbook. I found the work to be very rewarding and practical for my spiritual life. Over the years I have heard from many who have found great profit in going through this study. That is such a blessing to me. I am truly excited that you are embarking on this study through the Minor Prophets. This has been a rich and rewarding subject for me and I am confident that you will profit from the time you spend meditating on the concepts presented in the last twelve books of the Old Testament. The collection of twelve authors were indeed mighty messengers of God. Even though they lived centuries before us, their message needs to be heralded throughout our culture today.

As always there are several persons to thank in a project like this. Originally, I taught this material at Brownsburg Church of Christ in the summer of 2006. Many of the brethren there who sat in my classes each week have gone on to their reward. Their preparation, comments, and insight were of extreme value. I taught the material again for a Tuesday class a few years later after moving to work with the Kettering, Ohio Church of Christ (now known as Cornerstone Church of Christ). And now, in 2023, I am going through the material again, doing a complete revamp and update. Thanks again to the Cornerstone church for their help and support in going through this workbook. I need to also thank my wife, Becky, who always plays a very large role in editing the lesson text. Becky, your support, and encouragement keep me going even when it is difficult to write.

A hearty thank you also goes out to Randy Baughn from the Brownsburg Church of Christ in Indiana. Almost 20 years ago, he took time out of his busy schedule to help me design the cover for this book. Randy is a world-class photographer who worked for the Indianapolis Star for decades and has been a freelance photographer over the last decade or two. When it came time to update the cover for this workbook, there was no way I was going to replace his cover photo. He did a great job.

In this study I have labored hard to ensure that you not only get an idea of the contents of each book, but that you begin to grasp the political, economic, and social conditions of their time. When we begin to better understand their world, our eyes are opened to the urgency and passion of these men. Their message comes alive for us, and the obscurity that is so often associated with these books is lessened. I am sure that what you learn here will reward you with a wonderful treasure-trove of spiritual knowledge and wisdom.

May God bless you in all your spiritual pursuits.

Matthew Allen

May 2023

Table of Contents

Lesson 1

Introduction to the "Book of the Twelve"

F. W. Farrar called the Minor Prophets the "crown and flower of the Old Testament writings." Their extreme value and great profit can be easily overlooked. While a study on the Minor Prophets may not sound exactly interesting, once one delves into these brief books, written by obscure writers, much knowledge may be discerned. They are referred to as the Minor Prophets because of their brevity — not because of a lack of importance or authority in their content. These books are much shorter than what we refer to as the Major Prophets (Isaiah, Jeremiah, and Ezekiel). Taken individually, Isaiah, Jeremiah, and Ezekiel are longer than all twelve Minor Prophets put together. The twelve books we know today as the Minor Prophets were originally grouped together into a single "booklet" because of their small size. The Jews would have placed them together on one scroll because of their small size and the ease of keeping up with one scroll instead of twelve. The Minor Prophets were called the "Book of the Twelve" by Jews living in the first and second centuries.

Four Distinct Periods in Jewish History

PERIOD	CENTURY (B.C.)	BOOK	COMMENTS
Pre-Assyrian	Late 9th Early 8th	Obadiah Joel Jonah	Before the rise of Assyria to world-domination
Assyrian	8th Century	Amos Hosea Micah	Prophesied of coming destruction via Assyria & others
Babylonian	7th Century	Nahum Zephaniah Habakkuk	Babylon rapidly rising to power
Post-Exilic	Late 6th 5th Century	Haggai Zechariah Malachi	Babylon wanes, Rise of Persian domination

The Pre-Assyrian Period

The Pre-Assyrian Period includes writings between the mid-ninth century B.C. and the early eighth century B.C. **Obadiah, Joel**, and **Jonah** fit here. This would have been before Assyria rose to world domination and presented a major threat to God's people. These prophets warned the people of impending judgment.

The Assyrian Period

The Assyrian Period covers writings during the mid to late eighth century B.C. when Assyria was asserting its domination over countries to the east and north of Israel. As the century ended, Assyria threatened to move down the coast through Syria into the northern most reaches of the land of Israel. **Amos, Micah**, and **Hosea** are the books written during this time. Their message warns of the pending destruction of their country and people.

The Babylonian Period

The Babylonian Period covers the seventh century B.C. The Assyrians destroyed the northern ten tribes during the decade between 732-722. Samaria, the capitol, finally fell in 722. Almost as quickly as it rose to power, Assyria was gobbled up by the Babylonians in 612. **Nahum, Zephaniah**, and **Habakkuk** give us insight into the events and times of Judah during the rise of the Babylonians. In 587, Judah and Jerusalem were destroyed by the Babylonians, and the Israelites who were not killed were taken into captivity for seventy years. In these books there is a message of hope to assure the people that God would eventually allow a remnant to return to their homeland.

The Post-Exilic Period

The Post-Exilic Period gives us a glimpse of Israel during the years after the exile in Babylon. **Haggai, Zechariah**, and **Malachi** were written during this time. These prophets reminded the people that God was still the all-powerful God. These prophets also pointed out that the only reason Israel had been defeated was because of their rebellion against God.

The Arrangement of the Books

Arrangement of the Book of Twelve

HEBREW	CHRONOLOGICAL
Hosea	Obadiah
Joel	Joel
Amos	Jonah
Obadiah	Amos
Jonah	Hosea
Micah	Micah
Nahum	Nahum
Habakkuk	Zephaniah
Zephaniah	Habakkuk
Haggai	Haggai
Zechariah	Zechariah
Malachi	Malachi

Our English Bibles order these books the way that the Hebrews arranged them in their ancient text. They are not in chronological order. Why they are presented the way they are has been the subject of a great amount of speculation. One commentator suggests that Hosea was placed at the beginning because "it is the most comprehensive." Hosea's message applied mainly to Israel. Next, a prophet to Judah (Joel) was placed in the text. This was followed by a prophet to Israel, then to Judah, and so on and so forth. This method works for the first eight books. The final four books are said to be arranged chronologically.

Others believe that the first six books highlight the great sin of Israel, the next three discuss the punishment for that sin, and the final three books discuss the redemption of the people after the punishment that would take place. Perhaps the real reason for why the Hebrews arranged the books in the way they did will never be known.

This study takes the chronological perspective.

Political and Socioeconomic Concerns

Minor Prophets with their Historical Parallels

BOOK	DATES (B.C.)	BOOK
Obadiah	848-840	2 Chronicles 21:8-17; 2 Kings 8:20-22
Joel	835-796	Amos 1:2; 2 Kings 12:18; 2 Chronicles 24:23
Jonah	790-780	Deuteronomy 4:4-8; 2 Kings 14:25
Amos	760-750	2 Kings 14:23-25
Hosea	750-725	2 Chronicles 26-32; 30:1-12; Isaiah 36-37
Micah	735-700	Isaiah 2:2-5; 2 Kings 16:3; 2 Chronicles 28:2
Zephaniah	630-625	2 Kings 22-24
Nahum	630-612	2 Chronicles 34-35
Habakkuk	612-606	2 Kings 21.10-16; 2 Chronicles 33.10-16
Haggai	520	Ezra
Zechariah	520-518	Ezra
Malachi	445-432	Nehemiah 13; Ezra

These writings cover almost five centuries of history. Taken with the historical accounts we have in the Bible, we can develop a much better picture of how things were during the waning years of Israel and Judah. Self-satisfied, enjoying life, and hardened by sin, most of God's people settled for the sensual pleasures of idolatry and rejected the calls of a loving, compassionate God who wanted a relationship with people He called His own.

Over the one hundred twenty years before Solomon's death, the nation of Israel stood unified and reached its peak of power. It is no coincidence that during this time the nation was dedicated in its service and worship to God. During the later stages of Solomon's reign, he began to allow temples to be built to accommodate his many foreign wives in their idol worship. This set up the stage for rampant idolatry that would overtake the nation in the generations following his death.

A few decades after Solomon's death, the kingdom divided. The ten tribes in the north retained the name Israel and the southern two tribes began to refer to themselves as Judah. The Northern Kingdom instituted calf worship and the southern kingdom intermixed true worship to Jehovah along with worship to idols. The departure from worshipping Jehovah led to rampant corruption in all sectors of society. While enjoying very good economic conditions, the time of the prophets saw political upheaval, social justice ignored, and the poor being exploited by the rich. Soon after Solomon's death God rose up prophets like Elijah and Elisha in efforts to "wake up" the people from idolatry and social ills that were destroying them. After Elijah and Elisha came more prophets. Their message was trifold:

- Remind the children of Israel of the covenant they made with Jehovah upon the entrance to the Promised Land.
- Warn them of the certain, severe consequences to be brought upon them by God if they failed to repent.
- Provide glimpses of hope and restoration of a remnant after God's punishment and exile of the people.

Of the Minor Prophets, the early ones deal with God's judgment on Edom, punishment by God for continual rebellion, and repentance of the people of Nineveh, capital of Assyria. The repentance of a godless, barbaric people was a direct slap in the face to God's people who stubbornly refused to come back to God despite His repeated attempts to persuade them to return. The eighth century B.C. saw economically prosperous times for the people. While living in the luxury of the day, the calls for repentance by the prophets went largely ignored. **Obadiah**, **Joel**, and **Jonah** all prophesied during this time.

Amos, **Micah**, and **Hosea** lived during the Assyrian aggression. As the enemy crept in from the north, Israel (the northern ten tribes) found themselves in constant political upheaval. Assassination, corruption, and governmental disarray were common. As we move closer to the end, the northern kings were little more than puppet governments for the Assyrian invaders. The northern ten tribes were finally destroyed in 722. In the years leading up to the destruction of the northern ten tribes, Judah was not exempt from internal and external pressures. Israel, Egypt, and other nations constantly pressured Judah to join up with them to slow down the advances of the Assyrians. The prophets purpose during this time was to remind the people that instead of joining up with godless nations they had a responsibility to turn back to God, call on Him for deliverance, and trust in Him.

After the rapid decline of the Assyrian Empire, a new, more daunting foe came onto the scene. Babylon rose to world power after defeating the Assyrians in 612. Judah now finds itself in its final days as an independent nation. Political instability rules the day. Assassination, puppet governments, and high tribute to the enemy nation are all common during this time. These were dark days for Judah. **Nahum**, **Zephaniah**, and **Habakkuk** lived during the late seventh century build-up to Babylonian aggression. **Nahum** concentrates on the destruction of Nineveh (612), **Zephaniah** focuses on Judah's approaching doom, and **Habakkuk** speaks of Judah's punishment and the eventual destruction of the Babylonians.

Finally, the post-exilic prophets **Haggai**, **Zechariah**, and **Malachi** live in the period after the remnant returns to the homeland from seventy years of captivity. Through these prophets God provides spiritual hope and guidance to the exiles. The nation of Israel would never be independent and autonomous again. From this point on they would be ruled by foreign powers who looked at the Jews as little more than a conquered nation.

What can we learn from the Minor Prophets?

Romans 15:4 says, *for whatever was written in earlier times was written for our instruction, so that through perseverance and the encouragement of the Scriptures we might have hope.*

Later, Paul would write: *These things happened to them as examples, and they were written for our instruction, on whom the ends of the ages have come. So, whoever thinks he stands must be careful not to fall,* 1 Corinthians 10:11-12. There are several important themes and lessons we can take from these books. Consider these important concepts:

- **The moral, social, and economic conditions of God's people during a significant period of Israel's history**. We can gain a perspective in how immoral living, idolatry, and luxurious living caused the people of God to turn a deaf ear to His pleadings for repentance. There are several warnings to be gleaned from these verses – especially for Christians living in prosperous times.
- **God's interaction with nations other than Israel during Old Testament times**. God often raised up foreign nations to punish Israel for their sin. The sins of these heathen nations would not go unrecognized or unpunished by God.
- **God's call for repentance**. Although extremely sinful, God still held out for and called His people to repent. It is in these books where we see a wonderful example of His mercy, love, and concern for His people—despite their repulsive and unending rebellion.
- **God's certain punishment for wickedness**. God will not allow immorality, unfaithfulness, and rebellion to go unpunished.
- **Glimpses of the fulfillment of God's eternal plan through the Messiah and the church**. In these books we see foreshadowing and prophecies concerning the Messiah, the Holy Spirit, and the church. See Hosea 2:23; 11:1; 6:6; Joel 2:28-32; and Micah 5:2.

Prophetic viewpoints

Near View / Far View Perspectives of the Prophets

Judgment (End Times)

Christ (More Distant)

Captivity / Restoration (Near Future)

Israel / Judah (Prophets Own Time)

When studying the prophets, it is important to keep in mind the viewpoints they would use in their writing. Some people have referred to this as the *near-view/far-view* perspective of the prophets. Imagine standing on the summit of a mountain and looking at the peaks in the distance. Most often the prophets would look at the sins of their own day and warn against them. At other times, the prophet might look further out to the upcoming captivity of the people and God's restoration of the remnant during the post-exilic years. Some of their writings looked forward into the future-to the coming Messiah. And finally, some of their writing looks far out on the horizon, to the reign of Jesus over the church in His eternal kingdom. Understanding their different viewpoints is fundamental to coming to a better grasp of their writings.

For discussion

1. Why should we engage in lengthy studies of Old Testament books and concepts?

2. Why are some prophets called "major" and others "minor"?

3. What was the collection of Minor Prophets called by Jews living in the first and second centuries?

4. The four main periods the Minor Prophets cover are:

5. What was the tri-fold message of the prophets?

6. Briefly describe the political and socioeconomic times during the centuries the Minor Prophets lived.

7. Why is it important to know of the social and political conditions in this study? What would be some applications for our own generation?

8. What can God's dealings with nations other than Israel teach us today?

9. What can we learn about repentance from a study of the Minor Prophets?

10. Will God allow evil to go unpunished? How should this give today's Christian hope?

Obadiah: Servant of the Lord

Introduction

OBADIAH IS THE SHORTEST WRITING of the Minor Prophets. Obadiah's name, Servant of the LORD, was very common in Israel. The International Standard Bible Encyclopedia identifies thirteen different Obadiah's in the Old Testament. The Jewish Talmud holds that the prophet was the same Obadiah who was King Ahab's palace administrator, 1 Kings 18.3-16. Some suggest he is the man sent out by Jehoshaphat to teach God's law to the people in the hill country of Judah, 2 Chronicles 17.7. While some might make a case for either one of these, the fact is we know nothing about Obadiah beyond his name and that he received a revelation from God predicting the downfall of Edom.

The occasion of Obadiah's prophecy is difficult to ascertain. Suggested dates for the book range from the ninth century to the late fourth century B.C. The book names no king or date so the exact historical event is a matter of speculation. The Old Testament records four different occasions when Jerusalem suffered serious attacks and devastation:

- ~ 900 B.C. — 1 Kings 14.25-26; 2 Chronicles 12.1-12 — During Rehoboam's reign, Egyptian king Shishak invaded Jerusalem, seizing the treasuries in the temple and royal palace.
- ~ 845 B.C. — 2 Chronicles 21.16-17 — The Arabians and Philistines invade Judah, carrying off all the possessions in the palace and the sons and wives of the king.
- ~ 790 B.C. — 2 Kings 14.8-14; 2 Chronicles 25.17-24 — Jehoash's defeat of Amaziah and pillaging of the temple and the king's palace.
- ~ 587 B.C. — 2 Chronicles 36.11-21 — The destruction of Jerusalem by Nebuchadnezzar.

Today, many scholars prefer to place the writing of Obadiah around the end of Jerusalem/Judah in 597-587 B.C. Zedekiah was the last reigning king over Judah and after fleeing Jerusalem was captured near Jericho and returned to Nebuchadnezzar, 2 Kings 25.4-7. The Psalms, Ezekiel and Jeremiah all refer to Edomite involvement in the destruction of Jerusalem which seems to fit what Obadiah mentions in v. 10-14.

Other scholars prefer a much earlier date, ascribing Obadiah to be the earliest of the Minor Prophets, writing around 845 B.C. This perspective sees Obadiah as referring to a battle where Jerusalem was assaulted by the Arabians and Philistines during the reign of Jehoram in Judah and Joram (a.k.a Jehoram) in Israel. In this case, verses 10-14 would be linked to the historical account in 2 Kings 8.16-24 and 2 Chronicles 21:8-10, 16-17. Obadiah mentions foreigners entering the city gates working destruction and disaster. But there is no mention of the destruction of the temple or royal palace. Nothing is said about the people being carried into captivity in Babylon or a remnant heading for Egypt. It would seem reasonable that if such momentous and life-altering events were occurring during Obadiah's time, surely he would have mentioned this in his prophecy.

In this study, we will consider Obadiah's prophecy from the early date perspective.

The message of Obadiah is two-fold. The book opens with a decree of doom: Edom will be destroyed because of its pride and neglect of coming to the aid of Israel who had been attacked by foreigners. The second message focuses

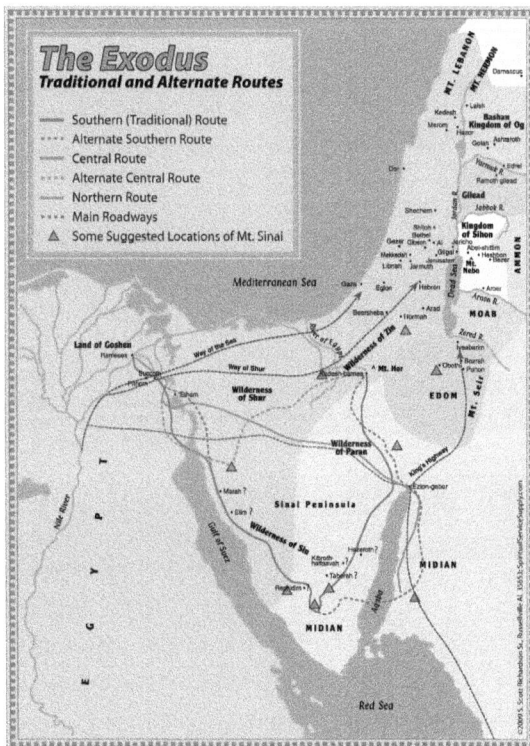

1—Edom resisted Israel's progress to the promised land. Edom resisted Israel's march to the promised land, Numbers 20. Map used by permission. S. Scott Richardson, Impressive Image Production, Athens, Alabama.

on the exaltation of Israel and the abasement of Edom (Mt. Seir) and the surrounding nations.

Edom's history

Edom was located south of the Dead Sea. It was a small country, measuring roughly seventy miles from north to south and only around fifteen miles east to west. The word "Edom" means red. This could be referring to the red sandstone cliffs that are a characteristic of the land Esau settled or it could be referring to the skin color of Esau. Most of the Edomites could be characterized as cliff-dwellers. Their capitol city of Sela (Petra in Greek) was hewn out of rock. They settled their territory around 1300 B.C., just before the Israelites arrived in the area.

The connection between Israel and Edom goes all the way back to Genesis with Esau and Jacob. From the womb disharmony characterized the relationship between Esau and Jacob, Genesis 25:22. Jacob stole Esau's birthright and later deceitfully obtained the blessing from his father Isaac. See Genesis 25 and 27. Because of this, Jacob fled for his life from Esau. Genesis 36:8-9 tells us that Esau became the father of the Edomites.

The running feud between Israel and Edom begins in earnest in Numbers 20 when Edom refuses to allow the Hebrew nation to pass through to the Promised Land. They always seemed to be a "thorn in the flesh" to Israel until they were finally brought down by David in the years after 1000 B.C. The subjugation of Edom allowed Israel to use and operate ports on the Red Sea, thus increasing their power and ability to trade with foreign nations. During this time Edom had no king—just a deputy appointed by Israel, 2 Kings 22:47. During Jehoram's reign Edom revolted. Now free of Judah's yoke, Edom returned to its former practice of aiding and abetting the enemies of Judah.

God sent Obadiah to warn of impending doom and punishment of the Edomites for their treatment of God's people. By 300 B.C. the Edomites had been captured by the Nabateans (a desert people), and what was left of them lived south of Judah. By 100 A.D. their country, language, and customs had completely disappeared, being absorbed by the Roman Empire. During the Roman Empire the Herods played a prominent role in regional government. We read of them during the days of Jesus and the early church. The Herods were descendants of the Edomites and were no friends to the people of God.

The World of Obadiah

TIME	ISRAEL		JUDAH	
	KING	PROPHET	KING	PROPHET
860				
	AHAB (873-853)	* Ahaziah (Ahab's son) ruled 853-852		
855		ELIJAH (874-850)	JEHOSOPHAT (871-848)	
850	JEHORAM (JORAM) (852-841)			
845			JEHORAM (848-841)	* Ahaziah (Jehoahaz) rules for 1 year (841-840)	OBADIAH (845-838)
			ATHALIAH (840-835)	* Athaliah was the queen mother
830				
		ELISHA (852-800)		
825	JEHU (841-814)		JOASH (835-796)	JOEL (836-822)
820				

The times of Obadiah

The years after the division of Israel and Judah were characterized by ongoing hostility. It subsided during the reign of Omri and Ahab in the north. As peace prevailed, the ruling families of each nation intermarried. Jehoshaphat (a relatively good king) chose Ahab's daughter (Athaliah) as a wife for his son Jehoram. This had extreme spiritual and national implications as the queen of Israel, Jezebel, was intent on pushing the worship of Baal on everyone. Her evil influence affected both nations. Jezebel's husband (Ahab, 873-853 B.C.) and two sons (Ahaziah, 853-852 B.C. and Jehoram, 852-841 B.C.) ruled in the north. Jezebel's son-in-law (Jehoram, 848-841 B.C.), grandson (Ahaziah, 841-840 B.C.), and daughter (Athaliah, 840-835 B.C.) ruled Judah. Largely because of the ruling class, the two countries, although at peace and economically prosperous, turned away from God. 2 Chronicles 21 describes the character of Jehoram of Judah. One of his first acts as king was to kill all six of his brothers and some of the princes of Israel to stave off any chance of having his reign put in jeopardy, 2 Chronicles 21:4. Verses 6-11 tell us more about his character and the subsequent punishment by God for the kingdom's rebellion.

> He walked in the way of the kings of Israel, just as the house of Ahab did (for Ahab's daughter was his wife), and he did evil in the sight of the Lord. Yet the Lord was not willing to destroy the house of David because of the covenant which He had made with David, and since He had promised to give a lamp to him and his sons forever. In his days Edom revolted against the rule of Judah and set up a king over themselves. Then Jehoram crossed over with his commanders and all his chariots with him. And he arose by night and struck down the

Edomites who were surrounding him and the commanders of the chariots. So Edom revolted against Judah to this day. Then Libnah revolted at the same time against his rule, because he had forsaken the Lord God of his fathers. Moreover, he made high places in the mountains of Judah, and caused the inhabitants of Jerusalem to play the harlot and led Judah astray.

Jehoram's actions prompted the judgment of God. The prophet Elijah sent a letter to the king prophesying about a coming affliction upon him and his family. He himself would be struck with many illnesses, the worst of which was a terrible, incurable intestinal condition. He would linger for two years before dying in great pain.

Verses sixteen and seventeen in 2 Chronicles 21 describe an attack on Jerusalem where the king's house was invaded. All the king's possessions and sons and wives were carried away by the Philistines and Arabs. The only son left to Jehoram was his youngest, Jehoahaz. Jehoahaz was also known as Ahaziah as the two names were interchangeable. When Jehoram died, no one mourned his death. A sad commentary is stated in 2 Chronicles 21:20: *He was thirty-two years old when he became king, and he reigned in Jerusalem eight years; and he departed with no one's regret, and they buried him in the city of David, but not in the tombs of the kings.* It is in the background of this attack on Jerusalem that Obadiah is written. Refer to Obadiah 10-11. Jerusalem had been humbled by this attack and Obadiah comes out to proclaim that the Lord's kingdom would ultimately triumph over those who had warred against it.

The Message of Obadiah

Judgment on Edom, v. 3-14

This book announces a report from the LORD concerning Edom. *Edom would be made small among the nations*, verse 2. The reasons for this are explained in detail in Obadiah's writing. Verses 3-9 speak of Edom's intense pride and verses 10-14 describe their treacherous behavior before God.

Intense Pride, v. 3-9

Pride has been the downfall of many a nation. We need to stand up and take notice from the lessons of the past, 2 Corinthians 10:6-12. The Edomites would fall because of their false sense of security in:

Their location, v. 3-4

The mountainous area of Edom made them feel secure from any invasion. The arid mountains, intense heat, lack of water, and rough terrain would make it difficult for any large army to come in. In addition, there were several fortified cities that would not be easily destroyed. The name of the capitol city, Sela, is translated The Rock. Because of the geographic features of their nation, they said to themselves: *who can bring me down to the ground?* God declared that he would bring them down.

Their money, v. 5-6

Edom possessed tremendous ore deposits and was on a major caravan route between the Middle East and the Far East. Edom grew rich from the tariffs imposed on caravans coming through their territory. Verse six describes the upcoming desolation: *how Esau will be ransacked, his hidden treasures searched out!* Edom would be completely emptied of any material prosperity.

Their alliances, v. 7

Because of its importance in trade, Edom had many commercial allies that it thought it could depend upon in case of attack. Military agreements had been made with other nations—providing a false sense of security that they were impregnable. God said that those at peace with them would deceive and overpower them.

Their wisdom and strength, v. 8-9

Some have pointed out that the Edomites were known for their wisdom in the ancient world. God would thwart their wise men with confusion. Their armies and special fighting men would be reduced to nothing. From the north to the south (Teman was thought to be in the south) their armies would be slaughtered.

There is much to learn from the Edomites fall from power. *The arrogance of your heart has deceived you,* v. 3. Worldly position, money, alliances, and personal strength provide no lasting security. The Edomites failure to recognize their dependence on God resulted in the loss of their own power and strength.

Transgressions against God, v. 10-14

Violence against Israel, v. 10-11

Edom had, almost from the beginning, been a continual enemy to God's people—the Israelites. While Israel was experiencing great problems from foreign invaders, Edom refused to come to their aid, *standing aloof.* They were just as guilty as the perpetrators of the crime. God says they would be destroyed forever. Within eighty years they would be conquered again by Judah during the reign of Amaziah. In the early 6th century B.C., Edom was invaded by the Chaldeans under Nebuchadnezzar, and later they were overtaken completely by the Arabic people known as the Nabateans. In fact, it was this group that drove them completely out of their homeland. In the second century B.C. the Macabees overtook this small remnant of Edomites and proselytized them into Judaism. Their culture and language completely disappeared.

Gloating over Israel's Misfortune, v. 12

The Edomites took great pleasure in the knowledge that those in Judah had suffered at the hands of their enemies. Note the usage of *day* in verse twelve. In the New American Standard Version, it is used four times, noting the devastation of destruction against God's people. Those who rejoice in the tragedy of others will have their own day of reckoning with the forces of God.

The Looting of Jerusalem, v. 13-14

These verses make it clear they had not only rejoiced in Jerusalem's peril but had joined the enemy in the looting of the city. As people fled Jerusalem, the Edomites stood at the crossroads, intercepting them to be captured and sold as slaves. Edom had long been known for its slave trade and took full advantage, selling their brethren into the slave trade as conquered people.

Edom would reap what it sowed, v. 15-16

It is Paul who wrote: *Do not be deceived, God is not mocked; for whatever a man sows, this he will also reap. For the one who sows to his own flesh will from the flesh reap corruption, but the one who sows to the Spirit will from the Spirit reap eternal life,* Galatians 6:7-8. Because of their transgressions, Edom would not escape the Day of the LORD.

The Day of the Lord

The term *Day of the LORD* is used throughout Scripture to bring people to an awareness of impending judgment from God. That judgment could be local, regional, or national. It is used throughout the prophetic writings of the Old Testament (Joel 1:15; 2:1, 10-11 and Isaiah 13:9-13). It is a day in which God makes Himself known by the righteous vengeance played out on His enemies. It is a day of terror and fear for the enemies of God, but a day of righteous redemption for those who are loyal to God. Ultimately, there is a Day of the LORD reserved for the future, in which God will call all creation together for judgment. This is the event in which all creation will give an account for the deeds done in the body, 2 Corinthians 5:9-10.

God's kingdom would ultimately triumph, v. 17-21

Verse seventeen begins the second section of Obadiah. It looks toward the future glory of Israel. God's kingdom would be established and Mt. Seir's (Edom) would be destroyed. The Mt. Zion as used in these verses refers to spiritual Jerusalem. The house of Jacob not only refers to his physical descendants but to those who would be redeemed under Christ. The house of Jacob and Joseph would be as a fire and burn Edom to stubble. Edom would be destroyed forever. Note the triumph of Mt. Zion in v. 17-18:

- Mt. Zion will be a place of deliverance or salvation, v. 17a.
- It will be set apart or holy, v. 17b.
- Those who dwell on Mt. Zion will be conferred with many possessions, v. 17c.
- Mt. Zion is characterized by unity, v. 18a. The house of Joseph and the house of Jacob are joined together.
- Mt. Zion is a place of victory, v. 18b. Edom would be reduced to stubble by the blazing fire and burning flame of God's people.

Mt. Seir was the tallest mountain in Edom, reaching almost five thousand feet in elevation. It was Edom's counterpart to Israel's Mt. Zion. Mt. Zion would conquer all her enemies including Mt. Seir. Verses 19-21 provide the details on how God's purposes would be carried out. Truly, God is in control of all the nations, their arrangements, size of territory, and even their very existence is in His control.

The message here is not so much about changing geography and worldly political power as it is that the captives of God's people would not be forgotten. The kingdom of God would continue to progress. It's inhabitants would not be on defense forever, but would, after the coming of the Christ, be the workers who expanded it in triumph, Acts 1.8.

Obadiah 17-21 is ultimately fulfilled in Christ

The destruction of Edom and its conquest by Judah are not all that is in this prophecy. These verses also look forward to a conquest which was ultimately fulfilled in Jesus Christ. Even as far back as Balaam we have glimpses of Christ subduing Edom through the power of His kingdom. In Numbers 24.15-24 Balaam prophesied: *I see him, but not now; I behold him, but not near; A star shall come forth from Jacob, A scepter shall rise from Israel.* The star is Jesus Christ. The scepter represents the power He would possess in His kingdom. Balaam goes on to say, *Edom shall be a possession, Seir, its enemies, also will be a possession, While Israel performs valiantly.* Obadiah speaks of Judah possessing Edom throughout verses 17-21.

Now, let's consider two more interesting passages, one in the Old Testament and the other in the New Testament.

> "In that day I will raise up the fallen booth of David, And wall up its breaches; I will also raise up its ruins And rebuild it as in the days of old; That they may possess the remnant of Edom And all the nations who are called by My name," Declares the Lord who does this, Amos 9.11-12.

Ultimately, Edom would become the conquered, the possession of others. It would be under the reign of Christ that this nation would become a possession. Note how James declares the prophecy of Amos finds its fulfillment in Christ. The bringing in of the Gentiles by the preaching of the apostles has been fulfilled through Christ:

> "With this the words of the Prophets agree, just as it is written, 'After these things I will return, And I will rebuild the tabernacle of David which has fallen, And I will rebuild its ruins, And I will restore it, So that the rest of mankind may seek the Lord, And all the Gentiles who are called by My name,' Says the Lord, who makes these things known from long ago, Acts 15.15-18.

For discussion

1. Obadiah's name means what? It is believed his book was written around:

2. What is the two-fold message of Obadiah?

3. Discuss Edom's relationship with Israel.

4. Discuss the importance of influence. As you answer, consider the devastating effects Jezebel had on Israel and Judah. What can we learn from this?

5. In what areas did Edom feel secure?

6. How can arrogance lead to a false sense of security?

7. Edom did nothing to come to the aid of Judah in their time of distress, verse 11. How did that make them guilty? Are there any New Testament principles we can consider? See James 4:17.

8. What is the Day of the LORD?

9. Why do you believe man has such difficulty in realizing that he will reap what he sows?

10. What does Mt. Zion refer to in Obadiah?

11. Explain how the prophecies in verses 17-21 have been fulfilled in Jesus Christ and His kingdom.

Joel 1.1—2.17:
The Day of the Lord is at Hand

Introduction

WE KNOW NOTHING OF JOEL'S PERSONAL HISTORY except that he was the son of Pethuel. In Hebrew his name means "Jehovah is God." Some suggest he was a priest or the son of a priest, but no firm evidence for this assertion exists. No king of Israel or Judah is mentioned in this book, which creates problems if we wish to place a fixed date on this writing. Some scholars date the book prior to 900 B.C., while others have it as late as 350 B.C. Since no king is mentioned, some argue that this gives greater evidence to a later date (after the remnant returns to Jerusalem and finds itself under the rule of foreign powers). While that makes sense, others date the book to the period between 835-817 B.C. which would have been during the minority of King Joash of Judah. Elders seem to be the real leaders in the country during Joel's writing and would have been looked at as the leaders of the nation during the formative years of the king. Because of this and the placement of this book in the Hebrew listing of the books, we will assume that the earlier date is the best date for Joel.

The days of Joash (835-796 B.C.)

The World of Joel

TIME	ISRAEL KING	ISRAEL PROPHET	JUDAH KING	JUDAH PROPHET
860				
850	JEHORAM (JORAM) (852-841)		JEHORAM (848-841)	
840			* Ahaziah (Jehoahaz) rules for 1 year (841-840)	OBADIAH (845-838)
			ATHALIAH (840-835)	* Athaliah was the queen mother
830	JEHU (841-814)	ELISHA (852-800)		JOEL (836-822)
830				
810			JOASH (835-796)	
800	JEHOAHAZ (814-798)			

During the reign of Jehoshaphat, the kingdoms of Judah and Israel maintained peaceful relations. To solidify this relationship, Ahab gave his daughter, Athaliah, to Jehoshaphat's son, Jehoram. After Jehoshaphat's death, Jehoram became king. He killed off all his brothers to solidify his power in the kingdom. Jehoram was a wicked king. He ruled eight years in Judah and was struck by God with a awful intestinal disease. After suffering for two years, his bowels came out and he died in great pain, 2 Chronicles 21:18-20. No one mourned his death, and he was not buried in the tombs of the kings.

Ahaziah, Jehoram's youngest son, was put into power at the age of twenty-two. He reigned one year in Jerusalem. His mother, Athaliah, counseled him to do wicked things which ultimately led to his destruction. By her influence, Ahaziah allied himself with Jehoram (Joram) of Israel. This alliance led to trouble as both countries went to war against Aram. Joram was wounded in battle and went to Jezreel to heal. Jehu had been anointed by God to cut off the house of Ahab (2 Chronicles 22:7) and killed Joram. While in Jezreel, Jehu found the princes of Judah, killed them, and pursued Ahaziah who fled to Samaria, only to be turned in to the forces of Jehu. As he escapes Jehu, he is mortally wounded and flees to Megiddo where he died, 2 Kings 9:27-28. Ahaziah was buried in Jerusalem in the royal cemetery.

After Ahaziah's death, there was no one left in his house to retain the power of the kingdom. Athaliah, the queen mother, rose and killed all the royal offspring. Had it not been for the providence of God working through Ahaziah's sister (Jehosheba), her vicious plan might have worked. Jehosheba took one year old Joash and his nurse and hid them from Athaliah for six years. Athaliah was overthrown and Joash became king at age seven, 2 Kings 11:17-21. In the early years of Joash's reign Jehoiada, the priest, played a significant role in influencing the people back to God, 2 Chronicles 23:16-21. With no king mentioned in Joel some speculate that it is during this time that Joel wrote his prophecy and addressed it to the people.

The Descendants of Athaliah

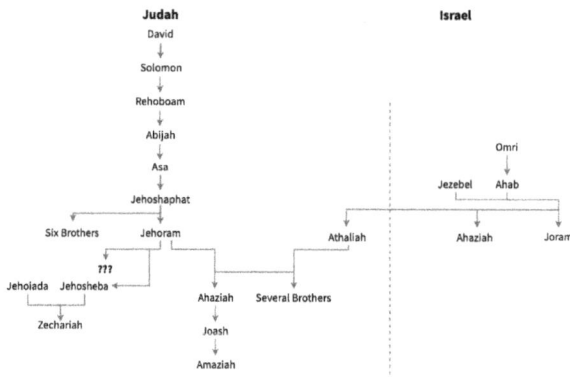

As Joash grew up and began to take the reins of the kingdom, he followed the Lord. In fact, he followed the Lord all the days of Jehoiada the priest. God blessed him and the kingdom of Judah. But after Jehoiada's death, Joash abandoned the house of God and went back to serving Asherim and other idols. In the historical account we read: *so wrath came upon Judah and Jerusalem for this their guilt. Yet He sent prophets to them to bring them back to the LORD; though they testified against them, they would not listen,* 2 Chronicles 24:18b-19.

The message of Joel

No matter the date of the writing, the message is timeless and applicable for all generations. There is much we can learn from this collection of writing. The book begins by Joel calling the people to action. An extreme plague of locusts had overtaken the land and their destruction was to be taken as a warning from God. Repentance was a matter of urgency—if they failed to repent, the "Day of the Lord" would come upon them. Repentance was something all needed to do—from the top to the bottom of society. This would be the only way to avoid judgment.

This lesson looks at the first thirty-seven verses of the book where Joel speaks. Here he talks of Judah's present circumstances, warns them of impending judgment, and encourages them to return to the Lord before it is too late. They were to return with *fasting, weeping, and mourning,* 2:12. Joel tells the people that God wanted their heart. He always has. We read, *rend your heart and not your garments." Now return to the Lord your God, For He is gracious and compassionate, Slow to anger, abounding in lovingkindness And relenting of evil,* 2:13.

The plague of locusts

All sectors of society are called to take notice and attention at the grievous situation facing Judah. The elders of the communities were the first to be summoned, and they would have been the ones over the people during the minority of King Joash. The old ones were asked to recall if they had ever seen it worse. The obvious answer is that they had not. The events they were facing were so monumental that they would need to pass along news of the devastation to the generations to come. In verse four we are finally told of what the occasion is. A swarm of locusts had enveloped itself all over the nation, wreaking havoc in its way. We are introduced to four stages of development in locusts. Each wave is followed by another one, only increasing the devastation.

- **The gnawing locust.** (Hatchling) This is the earliest part of development for the locust and it consumes the tender ground vegetation. At this point they look like ants.
- **The swarming locust.** (Hopper) The next stage of the development finds the locust maturing to where it completes the destruction of all tender vegetation.
- **The creeping locust**. (Winged Hopper) Now the locusts have grown where they attack the branches of trees and plants. Winged hoppers can move around 250 feet per hour and consume everything in their path.
- **The stripping locust.** (Mature Locust) At this point the locusts can strip even the bark off trees. There is little that can stop them as they move across the landscape.

Locusts look like large grasshoppers and mature desert locusts have a four-inch wingspan and bodies around three inches long. James Smith writes that what "typically distinguishes a true locust from a large grasshopper is behavior. When conditions are right, grasshoppers that normally act as solitary individuals begin to swarm. Great clouds of insects will rise during daylight hours in search of moist green vegetation. The sky can be blackened to an altitude of five thousand feet over tens of square miles. A swarm can contain over a billion creatures that all together can weigh more than three million pounds. When a species of grasshoppers exhibits this type of behavior, they are called locusts."[1] The message of verse four is that the locusts have wrought complete devastation. The leftovers have been consumed after each successive wave of infestation.

Not only were the elders and those who were engaged in community affairs to stand up and take notice to the words of Joel, but even the drunkards needed to wake up to what was going on around them. The locust plague was complete: they had laid the vineyards of Judah useless leaving no grapes to make wine. The locusts had stripped away the bark of the trees—exposing the white inner part of the tree, 1:7. Priests are called upon to weep and wail before God—there is nothing left for them to offer up before the Lord. The locust plague affected all facets of society. Along with the devastation created by the locusts, it appears that a drought might have settled in. The Hebrew word *yabhash* (dry up, wither) is used seven times in Joel 1.

The first thirteen verses leave us with unanswered questions. As Joel describes the devastation in the first part of chapter one, is he describing actual events that had just happened, or is he looking ahead to some future judgment? Should this be taken as a literal army of locusts, or is this language symbolic of invading armies at some point in the future? It is best to let the text speak for itself. The language indicates that an actual horde of locusts had devastated the land in the months/years preceding Joel's writing. It was something intended as a wake-up call; something used by God to urge His people toward repentance. That these are actual events is seen in reading 1:16-20.

A Call to Repentance in Joel 1

- 1.2: Elders & all people told to tell future generations of the devastation
- 1.5: Drunkards were to weep and wail
- 1.8-9: Priests were to mourn
- 1.11: Farmers were to be ashamed
- 1.13: Priests were to lament and wail

The call to repentance

Beginning in verse fourteen the priests are urged to proclaim a fast, gather the people together, and cry out to God. It is implied that if they will do this, and do it sincerely, God will listen and relent from a future day of punishment and judgment. While things were not good in Judah at the time of Joel's writing, they could potentially get worse, much worse! The *day of the Lord*, 1:15, would be complete and total devastation would come on those who turned their backs on God. They needed to repent while there was still time. The events surrounding them should have been cause enough for repentance.

At this point Judah was suffering:

- 1:16 — food had been cut off.
- 1:17 — seeds could not grow because of lack of water.
- 1:17 — desolate storehouses and dried up grain.
- 1:18 — livestock suffered because of lack of pasture and moisture.
- 1:19-20 —fire destroyed grazing land and pastures in the wilderness.

It is in cases such as this that man has only one place to turn: God. It is in natural disasters that we often realize how small we are and our great dependence on God for the necessities of life. Our sterilized life here in America may shroud this reality, but there are events in life that come along to shock us back to reality—everything we have is from and because of God. We need to draw near to Him with reverence and humility.

A day of destruction is coming

The first verses of chapter two introduce us to a very urgent warning. The blowing of a trumpet was a sound of warning or alarm. The Day of the Lord was near. The people needed to return to God for protection and deliverance from the enemy.

As we go throughout verses two through eleven, a future day of gloom and punishment is described. The locust plague should have gotten their attention. Just as the locust plague had been unusual in its severity and destruction, so would the Day of the Lord.

> There has never been anything like it, Nor will there be again after it, 2:2.

On the Day of the Lord, the people are powerless to stop the enemy from overtaking them. All they can do is hide and watch the land being destroyed in front of their eyes:

> The land is like the garden of Eden before them but a desolate wilderness behind them, 2:3.

Not only is the army unstoppable, but Joel also describes the individual strength of the warriors. They can run, climb, march straight toward their target, enter windows like thieves, and fulfill their mission of destruction and death. Nothing can stop them.

The figurative words in verse ten are used to describe the complete and total destruction that would take place. In fact, Jeremiah, Ezekiel, Amos, and even Jesus used this type of language to describe the destruction that took place on *the Day of the Lord*. (Keep in mind there are several Days of the Lord in Scripture—they do not all refer to the end of time. This is a day that is used to describe days when God would pour out His vengeance on those who rebel against Him.) ...*The day of the Lord is indeed great and very awesome, and who can endure it?* (2:11)

The people needed to repent to stave off disaster. Not only did the people need to realize their great dependence upon God, but they also needed to sincerely change their ways. Complete, radical change was necessary to avert the terrible consequences to come. *Who knows whether He will not turn and relent and leave a blessing behind Him*, 2:14. The priests are encouraged to blow a trumpet again. This time, not for a warning, but it was to be blown for a gathering of the people to cry out to God for deliverance. If they would turn their hearts to God, it is implied that He would hear their prayers and relent from the impending doom.

The Day of the Lord in the Minor Prophets

REFERENCE	DESCRIPTION
Joel 1:15	*It is near. Will come as destruction.*
Joel 2:1	*It is near*
Joel 2:11	*It is very awesome. Who can endure it?*
Joel 2:31	*awesome*
Amos 5:18	*darkness, ...not light*
Amos 5:20	*gloom, with no brightness in it*
Obadiah 15	*draws near on all the nations*
Zephaniah 1:7	*is near...*
Zephaniah 1:14	*is near and coming very quickly*
Malachi 4:5	*a great and terrible day*

Lessons for Today

God can use natural events to motivate mankind to repentance

There can be little doubt that God brought about the locust plague as a warning to His people. They needed to look at the events from a spiritual perspective. Mankind is not as big and powerful as he may think, and it is often events from nature that vividly remind us of this fact. While God may not use every natural calamity to cause mankind to be more alert about His presence, we must not deny God the possibility of using such events to stir mankind to a greater awareness of Him. When these things happen, we become acutely aware of the fragility of life and the finality of death. Let us use these times as motivation to draw near to God, realize our dependence upon Him, and repent of sin.

There is great power in fasting and corporate prayer during a time of crisis

In Joel 1:14 the priests are urged to consecrate a fast and proclaim a solemn gathering of God's people. They were to cry out to God for deliverance. During biblical times fasting was evidence of grief and anguish. It was done in a way to "pacify" the anger of God in hopes that He would relent from punishment. Their prayer and fasting were to come from the heart—realizing their total dependence upon God. It is in these times that God listens. He wants us to reach out to Him in total trust and confidence. Do we realize the power in fasting and corporate prayer that is available to us today? James writes,

> Is anyone among you suffering? Then he must pray. Is anyone cheerful? He is to sing praises. Is anyone among you sick? Then he must call for the elders of the church and they are to pray over him, anointing him with oil in the name of the Lord; and the prayer offered in faith will restore the one who is sick, and the Lord will raise him up, and if he has committed sins, they will be forgiven him. Therefore, confess your sins to one another, and pray for one another so that you may be healed. The effective prayer of a righteous man can accomplish much, James 5:13-16.

The power of both individual and corporate prayer is seen in these verses. Let us turn to God when times of calamity befall us. He will be there for us. There is great power in prayer!

God expects true repentance ... not lip service

Even now—this is the Lord's declaration—turn to me with all your heart, with fasting, weeping, and mourning. Tear your hearts, not just your clothes, and return to the Lord your God, 2:12-13a. See here how it is God who is calling them to repent. Does this not teach us something special about the God we serve? What a great and awesome God He is in that He is always holding out, hoping, asking us to move toward Him.

In this is a great lesson on repentance. It involves sweeping change—not just the making of empty promises or vain words uttered up in hopes that He will relent. True repentance involves a complete and total surrender to God. What does 2:12 teach us about true repentance?

True repentance involves a sense of urgency to act

This is indicated by the usage of the word "now" in the text. When one realizes the reality of punishment to come and the possibility that it could come at any time, there will be little delay in getting matters in the open before God. A person who moves in genuine repentance understands that time is precious and one moment spent outside of a relationship with God is one moment too long.

True repentance involves a desire to return to God

In the case of Joel's day God's people had entered a covenant relationship with God. Through the worship of idols, trust in human alliances, and turning their back on God, they had not lived up to their side of the covenant. God is calling them to do what is necessary to return. We are the ones who destroy the connection with God through our sinful behavior, yet

The Nature of God in Joel 2:13

GOD IS
gracious
compassionate
slow to anger
abounding in lovingkindness
relenting of evil

God always calls us back so that the relationship can be restored to its former quality.

True repentance comes from the heart

Tear your hearts, not just your clothes, and return to the Lord your God, 2:13. Repentance must go further than fear of punishment and/or confession of sin. It is a complete and total change. It is an inward change of the soul, and while it begins in the mind, it reveals itself outwardly.

True repentance will be seen in our actions

Fasting, weeping, and mourning are all evidence of true, genuine repentance. However, these things do not profit the person who has not changed his will. Israel was called upon to change their will and demonstrate it in a national assembly. They needed to show God they were sorrowful for their own sin, demonstrate their submission to Him, and earnestly plead for God to turn back from his impending destruction. Fruits of repentance will be seen when it is genuine and true. See Matthew 3:8.

How great and awesome is the God we serve! Verse thirteen tells us some incredible things and reasons why we should move to Him in repentance. If the people would follow through, God would relent from the terrible Day of the Lord Joel warned about in chapter two.

For discussion

1. In Hebrew what does Joel mean?

2. This book best fits in what time?

3. Describe the turmoil in Judah's royal family in the years before Joash became an adult.

4. The four stages of locust development are described in 1:4. What are they and describe the potential for destruction at each stage.

   a)

   b)

   c)

   d)

5. In Chapter 1 do you believe Joel is describing an actual locust infestation or some future judgment? Why?

6. Describe the conditions found in Judah at the time of Joel's writing.

7. What can a time of crisis and devastation teach us?

8. What would happen on the Day of the Lord?

9. How can natural calamity motivate mankind to repentance?

10. What was the purpose of fasting during biblical times?

11. Why is repentance often difficult?

12. What four things are involved in true repentance?

a)

b)

c)

d)

13. What are five ways God is described in 2:13? What do each one of
    these mean to you?

Chapter Endnotes
1   Smith, James E., *The Minor Prophets,* p. 67.

Joel 2.18-3.21:
The Need for True Repentance

Introduction

THE FIRST HALF OF JOEL speaks of a locust plague that had devastated
Judah. The people are urged to repent and turn to God before the coming
of the great Day of the Lord. Because of the destructive power of the locust
plague, every facet of society had been affected. The people were urged to
turn to God, seek His deliverance, and repent from the heart.

2:18-27: The blessings of repentance

Beginning in verse eighteen and continuing through verse twenty we can
imply that the people repented. Sometimes it takes people reaching the
lowest depths to be shaken to the point of repentance. Could that have been
what happened here? In these verses God promises to restore grain, wine,
and oil to the point that they would be satisfied in full, 2:19. God promises
that His people will never be a reproach among the nations again. According
to some commentators, the *northerner* mentioned in 2:20 is the locust
plague. God would drive the plague into desert areas, toward the eastern
(Dead) sea, and the western (Mediterranean) sea. The death of so many
locusts at the same time would cause a terrible stench. Just as God brought
about the locust plague to stimulate the people to repentance, when they
followed through, He removed the plague to give His people relief.

Verses twenty-one through twenty-seven describe in detail the complete
restoration of the people's material blessings. God promised to make up for
the years that the locusts had destroyed their crops so that the people would
praise the name of God. The contrast between 1:14-20 with 2:21-27 could
not be greater. Weeping, mourning, and lamenting over sin are given over to
rejoicing, relief, and restoration.

2:28-32: The outpouring of the Spirit

This is a good time to review the near view / far view section in the first
lesson that discusses the way the prophets looked forward to future events.
In this part of Joel, the prophet is looking out into the distance to the
establishment of the church of Jesus Christ. After the restoration of physical
blessings, Joel speaks of the outpouring of the Spirit in verse twenty-eight.

On the Day of Pentecost, Peter points to this passage, outlining its fulfillment by the gift of the Holy Spirit, Acts 2:17-21.

The gift of the Holy Spirit is the Spirit Himself, who in our baptism, takes up residence in our heart bringing spiritual life and eternal salvation, Titus 3.4-6. The gift is available to all: men, women, old, young, rich, poor, slave, free, etc., see Acts 2.38, 5.32; Joel 2.32a. This is the main emphasis of the Acts 2 passage.

To prove the validity of the salvation message on Pentecost, Peter and the eleven other apostles received the ability to work miraculous signs and wonders. Later, to prove salvation was for the Gentiles, Cornelius and his family received miraculous gifts of the Spirit in Acts 10. Philip the evangelist had four daughters who prophesied through the Spirit, Acts 21:9. This is in great contrast to the Old Testament times where only certain ones received miraculous gifts of the Spirit to lead God's people, etc. Supernatural spiritual gifts were a first century phenomenon. In 1 Corinthians 13:8, Paul tells us that these would pass away.

Symbolic Language Concerning the Day of the Lord

REFERENCE	OBSERVATIONS
Isaiah 13:10	sun, moon, stars darkened
Isaiah 34:4	heavens wither away; sky rolled up as a scroll
Jeremiah 4:23	earth loses form; is void; heavens have no light
Ezekiel 32:1-8	sun, moon, stars darkened
Amos 8:9	sun goes down at noon; earth dark in broad daylight
Matthew 24:29	sun and moon darkened; stars fall from sky
Luke 21:25	signs in the sun, moon, stars; roaring sea & waves
Revelation 6:12-13	sun becomes black; moon turns red like blood; stars fall to earth

2:30-32: A Time of Judgment

Verses thirty through thirty-two speak of a coming judgment by God. The coming age of the church would also include a time of judgment. Most Jews rejected Jesus Christ and His message. These would be left to experience the great Day of the Lord. *Wonders in the sky* is like the language Jesus used in Matthew 24 in describing events just prior to the destruction of Jerusalem in 70 A.D., Matthew 24:29. *Blood, fire, and smoke* are all representative of the destruction the Jews suffered and indicate the tremendous price they paid for rejecting God. This type of language is quite common among the prophets as they look for vivid ways to describe the power and effects of the judgment. One can find similar language speaking of the Day of the Lord in Isaiah, Jeremiah, Ezekiel, and Amos. We also see it used in Revelation speaking of the destruction of those who oppressed and killed the early Christians.

There can be little doubt that the Day of the Lord mentioned in Joel 2 references the destruction of Jerusalem in 70 A.D. Most Jews living in this time could not imagine any other way than for God to operate through the physical nation of the Jews. Not only were they not open to conforming to God's new way, but they also actively sought the destruction of those in the church who clearly taught that the law had been fulfilled through Jesus Christ. The destruction of Jerusalem was complete and total. Some have suggested that the destruction of Jerusalem is only a forerunner of the final judgment when God will judge all those who reject Jesus Christ and His way.

Verse thirty-two speaks of hope of deliverance from this Day of Judgment. *Whoever calls on the name of the Lord will be delivered....* This has a dual meaning. Spiritually, the call of salvation was available to everyone. Calling on the name of the Lord involves faith, repentance, and baptism. This is the only way to avoid the great Day of the Lord at the end of time. We must prepare for that event now.

Physically, those living in and around Jerusalem were warned to flee Jerusalem when they saw various signs coming to pass as outlined by Jesus in Matthew 24:15-21. Many Christians followed through and escaped to the east to Pella during Jerusalem's overthrow by the Romans. The Mount Zion and Jerusalem in verse thirty-two are best understood in a spiritual context. They are used to describe the spiritual dwelling place of God and His people. See also Hebrews 12:22-23. Obadiah also mentioned about those who had escaped the judgment of God as dwelling on Mount Zion. Obadiah verse 17 says, *But on Mount Zion there will be those who escape, and it will be holy....*

3:1-16a: The enemies of God will be destroyed

Chapter three opens with the statement, *for behold, in those days and at that time....* This connects the chapter with the events of the last part of chapter two. A time period is under consideration here, not a specific point in history which makes it impossible to tie in the prophecy with specific events. It is important to read chapter three with a spiritual view in application. Tying in physical events and fulfillments will cause one to lose the point: God's people (spiritual Israel) would experience great and wonderful blessings while the enemies of God would suffer the consequences of their evil rebellion. For example, verse two mentions how God will bring all the nations to the valley of Jehoshaphat and judge them there. How is a physical application possible? How could all nations be literally gathered in one valley? Is there room for such?

Obviously, the best explanation is something symbolic. 2 Chronicles 20:1-30 speaks of a battle where enemy forces were destroyed by God. This valley of Jehoshaphat represents the ultimate defeat of God's enemies and the deliverance of His chosen ones. An interesting twist on this is that in Hebrew, Jehoshaphat literally means "Jehovah judges." Understanding this "valley" in verse two may help us better understand the "valley of decision" mentioned in verse fourteen. The "valley" is symbolic in describing a time of God's judgment against His enemies. Their misdeeds will not go unpunished. There seems to be an overlying principle here and throughout God's word: God will be there for His people, and He will deal out vengeance on those who seek harm on them. See Psalm 94:1-4; Nahum 1:2-3; and Romans 12:18-19.

3:3-10: Judgment on Israel's Oppressors

In verses three through eight God is listing out His judgment on all those who persecuted God's people and sold them into slavery. The judgment will be swift and certain. It is extremely difficult to place a physical date of fulfillment on these verses. One reason is because of what we read in verse one that ties the contents of this chapter to the time of the outpouring of the Spirit. We have no historical account of these events taking place after the first century. We do know that in the period after Joel that Uzziah and Hezekiah fought against the Philistines. Secular history also points to a war between the Maccabeans and Philistines in the centuries just before Jesus. During this time, Phoenicia was totally dominated by Judea and the Phoenicians were subdued by Alexander in 332 B.C. The best interpretation seems to be that God will render judgment on those who oppress and despise His people. This is certain. Verse eight concludes with the statement, *for the Lord has spoken.*

In verses nine and ten the focus shifts back to a universal judgment on all the nations as outlined in verse two. The enemies of God are told to prepare themselves for war. They are going to war with the forces of God in the valley where God judges. In essence God is calling them to their doom. Smith notes several different pictures of God's judgment as seen in verses twelve through fifteen.

Differing Scenes of Judgment in Joel 3.12-15

REFERENCE	OBSERVATIONS
Joel 3:12	*a courtroom*
Joel 3:13	*a great and ripe harvest*
Joel 3:14	*a noisy, apprehensive multitude*
Joel 3:15	*sun, moon, and stars darken*

3:12-15: The courtroom of God's judgment

3:12: A Courtroom

The location of this courtroom is the "Valley of Jehoshaphat." From there God will sit to *judge All the surrounding nations.* The Hebrew word that is translated "to judge" means to pronounce a sentence and execute judgment. Those who warred against God and His ways would suffer the consequences of total annihilation from the forces of God.

3:13: A great harvest

Joel points to a ripe harvest and a full wine press. The nations were ripe for judgment and had been gathered for God to execute justice. Just as grain would be threshed and grapes smashed so would be the punishment exacted by God. This punishment would be just because *the vats overflow, for their wickedness is great,* 3:13.

3:14: Multitudes of people would be at this great judgment

Many people would be gathered, and the number would be great as the word "multitudes" is repeated in this passage. This represents the largest possible gathering of people. The Hebrew wording points to a noisy, tumultuous crowd that is agitated and anxious. They are here to experience the Day of the Lord.

3:15: The heavens give no light

The sun, moon, and stars grow dark. This terminology always accompanies the great judgment of God. All of creation seems to tremble at the coming judgment and vengeance of God. If the powerful forces of nature pause in recognition of the power of God, who is man to think that he can have success against the righteous retribution of God?

3:16a: God's judgment is terrifying

The pending judgment of God and the execution of the sentence strikes great terror. So much, in fact, that *The Lord roars from Zion and utters His voice from Jerusalem, And the heavens and the earth tremble...*, 3:16a. This reminds us of the words of the Hebrew writer who speaks of *a terrifying expectation of judgment and the fury of a fire which will consume the adversaries. For we know Him who said, "Vengeance is Mine, I will repay." And again, "The Lord will judge His people." It is a terrifying thing to fall into the hands of the living God,* Hebrews 10:27, 30-31.

3.16b-21: The blessings of being in Mount Zion

While this judgment is going on, God's people will find refuge. *But the Lord is a refuge for His people and a stronghold to the sons of Israel,* 3:16b. He sustains His people through His grace, mercy, and love. Because of God's judgment and safety for His people, all will know that Jehovah is God. Note how in 3:17 God says, *I am the LORD* **your** (emphasis added) *God.* See the special relationship God has with His people. Again, it is important to view Jerusalem and Zion in a spiritual sense here. It is a mighty city where no stranger will pass through it. It is a special place reserved only for the redeemed.

At the beginning of verse eighteen we find the phrase *in that day.* The context suggests that day is during the time after the church has been established. Joel is communicating these things in what we might call "Old Testament Language." He is speaking in terms that the people of His day would readily understand. It is important to view these verses with this in mind. During Joel's time, God's people lived in an agrarian society, so he speaks of the bounty of the times to come in terms they would readily understand:

- Freshly pressed grape juice in abundance.
- No scarcity of milk.
- Streams flowing with fresh, abundant water.

During Old Testament times, physical images were often used to portray spiritual blessings in the age to come. Smith writes, "Old Testament prophecy symbolized the spiritual blessings of the New Covenant age."

The people of Joel's day would have associated Edom and Egypt with the great enemies of God and His people. While the people of God will be blessed immensely, enjoying peace and security, those who stand against God will become a waste and a desolate wilderness. This would happen because of their violence against God's people. God says that Judah would be inhabited forever for all generations. The people of Joel's day would have interpreted this as a great contrast between eternal life and death. These verses speak of the day when God would establish a spiritual nation (the church) and dwell among them. The ungodly would be judged and destroyed for their wickedness.

Lessons for Today

God wants a relationship with His people

Joel 2:26-27 speaks of God's great desire to have a relationship with His creation: mankind. God wants to bless His people bountifully and has through Jesus Christ, Ephesians 1:3-4. Indeed, God has dealt wondrously with us, 2:26. In verse twenty-seven God identifies His desire to be in a personal relationship with us, *I am the Lord,* **your** *God.* It is as if God always has His hand reaching out to us, earnestly desiring us to draw near to Him. He holds out for our repentance and cannot wait to dispense his lovingkindness and mercy upon us. How thankful are we that we serve a God who is willing to take a personal interest in every person living on the face of the earth? See Romans 5:8-10; Psalm 103:1-13; and John 3:16. The blessings that God bestows on us, especially the spiritual, are dependent on our repentance and obedience to His expectations.

God shows His mercy and grace by offering mankind an escape from the great and terrible Day of the Lord

Joel 2:32 speaks of those who are delivered from destruction. Just as God promised deliverance from those who would have to experience the destruction of Jerusalem in 70 A. D., so He promises deliverance from the great Day of the Lord at the end of time. This deliverance comes through Jesus Christ and the salvation found through Him. The final judgment will come, Hebrews 9:27; 2 Corinthians 5:9-10. Deliverance from this great day will only be possible during a person's physical life. There will be no escape after death or when the Lord returns to execute judgment.

God will always protect His people

This is an underlying theme in the second half of this book. Even if God's people find themselves subjected to suffering and persecution during this life, they can rest assured that God will not leave the wicked unpunished. This is also one of the principal messages of Revelation. God and His people will be victorious. There are many passages that speak of God as our Rock of refuge. See Psalm 61:1-8 and 62:1-9. Those who trust in Him will be delivered, and even if they lose their physical life, eternal life will be theirs.

For discussion

1. To what extent did God promise to restore the physical needs of the people (2:19)?

2. Describe the contrast between 1:14-20 and 2:21-27.

3. How does the near view / far view understanding of how the prophets looked to future events help you to better understand 2:28-3:17?

4. When was 2:28-29 fulfilled? Cite scripture for your answer.

5. The Day of the Lord in 2:30-32 refers to what event?

6. What is involved in calling on the name of the Lord?

7. How are Mount Zion and Jerusalem used in the context of Joel?

8. What is the Valley of Jehoshaphat in 3:2?

9. What does Jehoshaphat mean in Hebrew?

10. Why is it so difficult to link 3:3-8 with specific events in history?

12. Describe the judgment in 3:12-16a.

13. Why is it important to view 3:17-21 in the context of how the people of Joel's day would understand it?

14. What are some additional lessons you can learn from this lesson on Joel?

Jonah 1-2:
Jonah and the Great Fish

Introduction

WITHOUT A DOUBT Jonah is one of the most debated books within the Minor Prophets. Should its contents be treated historically or as an allegory? Did the prophet really spend three days and nights inside the belly of a great fish? Why all the miracles within such a short book? Even with all the controversy the book has been called a masterpiece. Jonah was the son of Amittai, and his name comes from the Hebrew word "dove." His home was the small village of Gath-hepher, located a few miles northeast of Nazareth.

Jonah lived and prophesied during the reign of Jeroboam II in Israel (793-753 B.C.). Jeroboam II brought the nation of Israel back to a level of political and economic stability and power that had not been seen since the reign of David, almost two hundred years before. Some have suggested Jonah was the most prestigious prophet of his day. He is mentioned as prophesying for the king in 2 Kings 14:25. Fiercely patriotic of his homeland, Jonah could not understand God's plan of saving the Ninevites if they repented.

The world of Jonah

As mentioned above, the northern ten tribes of Israel experienced a period of great economic and political strength during the eighth century B.C.

The World of Jonah

TIME	ISRAEL			JUDAH		
	KING		PROPHET	KING		PROPHET
810						
	JEHOAHAZ (814-798)		ELISHA (852-800)	JOASH (835-796)		
800						
790						
780	JEHOASH (JOASH) (798-782)					
				AMAZIAH (796-767)		
770	JEROBOAM II (793-753)	* Jeroboam II was co-regent with Joash for 11 years.	JONAH (780-760)			
760				UZZIAH (792-740)	* Uzziah was co-regent with Amaziah for 25 years.	
						ISAIAH (762-690)
750			AMOS (760-750)			

Jeroboam II's father, Jehoash had begun a series of wars against Aram (Syria) and 2 Kings 13:14-25 says Jehoash retook several towns that Aram had taken from Israel. After Jehoash's death, Jeroboam II continued the national expansion restoring the borders of Israel to what they were during the reign of David and Solomon. Almost all of Aram was conquered, including Damascus. Moab and Ammon were also subjected to the rule of Israel during this period. Jeroboam II launched expensive building projects around Samaria, including fortifying the city with a double wall thirty-three feet in width. These fortifications were so strong that in 722 B.C. it took the Assyrians three years to conquer the city, 2 Kings 17:5.

There was a strong sense of pride in the country during this time, and along with the good economic times the importance of art and décor arose. Unger's Bible Dictionary refers to a "blossoming of the arts in this prosperous era." There were many great houses, and the rich found themselves in luxury with both summer and winter homes. The good and prosperous times allowed for much banqueting and indulgence, but with little regard for the poor and underprivileged. During this time, religious practice would have been more ritualistic than from the heart: a problem which would be dealt with by Amos who would come on the scene a few years after Jonah.

The Assyrians were the most powerful nation and the greatest enemy of Israel. They were ruthless warriors who inflicted great suffering on the nations they conquered. The Assyrians were so brutal that they were known to bash skulls and decapitate victims who had presumably surrendered. They were known to carry off women and children while torturing and executing the men left behind. Perhaps no nation before the Assyrians had become so ungodly, calloused, and cruel. The Assyrian king Ashurnasirpal II, (883-859 B.C.) is said to have written:

> I stormed the mountain peaks and took them. In the midst of the mighty mountains, I slaughtered them; with their blood I dyed the mountain red like wool. With the rest of them I darkened the gullies and the precipices of the mountains. I carried off their spoil and their possessions. The heads of their warriors I cut off, and I formed them into a pillar over against their city; their young men and their maidens I burned in the fire! I built a pillar over against the city gates, and I flayed all the chief men who had revolted, and I covered the pillar with their skins; some I walled up within the pillar, some I impaled upon the pillar on stakes, and others I bound to stakes round about the pillar.[1]

These facts should help the reader to better understand at least some of the rationale behind Jonah's initial refusal to go to Nineveh. Human nature wants quick and immediate destruction of its enemies and has a hard time understanding how God can accept the repentance of such a cruel people.

As Israel's prosperity rose, Assyria battled with internal strife, including the Armenians who lived near the Caspian Sea. During this time, the power of the king was greatly diminished, and the provincial governors wielded great influence over government. There were no large campaigns against foreign nations during this time. During the 760's B.C., Assyria found itself in the middle of a great famine, and in 765 B.C. and again in 759 B.C. great plagues spread throughout the nation. On January 15, 763 B.C., there was a total eclipse of the sun, which always gave the ancients great cause for alarm. As far back as the 790's, there had been a push for monotheism within Assyria. All or some of these factors could explain the readiness of the people to repent when Jonah came calling in chapter three of his book.

The message of Jonah

The main theme of the book is repentance. God has always wanted all men to repent and turn to Him. His concern is for all, and he is willing that no one perish, 2 Peter 3:9. God's universal love and care is seen in the book. *Should I not have compassion on Nineveh, the great city in which there are more than 120,000 persons who do not know the difference between their right and left hand, as well as many animals?* Jonah 4:11. Some have suggested that the message of repentance should have served as a wake-up call for Israel. Imagine a heathen nation, so cruel and brutal who overwhelmingly responds to God's call for repentance. Contrast that to the absence of repentance from the nation of Israel. Israel had been constantly cared for by God, recipients of His divine favor, and had witnessed God's great miracles and works.

A sub-theme in the book is that **God reigns supreme over all nations**. All people everywhere are subject to His power, authority, and judgment. When calling Jonah to go to Nineveh, God said that *their wickedness had come up before Him,* Jonah 1:2. If the Assyrian people wanted their lives spared, they were required to humble themselves before God. Hailey points out that this book is sometimes referred to as "the forerunner of the universal gospel message which would be carried to all the heathen world."[2]

Should we treat the contents and message of Jonah as historical or as an allegory? If we let Scripture speak for itself, this message will be seen as historical. What the Bible says happened, happened. The miracles in this book are no different from any other book in the Bible. If we deny those contained in this book, what is to stop us from explaining away the resurrection of Jesus, the miracles wrought by the apostles, and all the other signs and wonders within the pages of God's word?

Jonah disregards God's message and flees to Tarshish

The book opens with a simple declarative statement. God came to Jonah, told him to go to Nineveh and cry out against it. This was most likely a shock for Jonah as it was unusual for prophets to go to foreign cities and pronounce God's judgment upon them. Nineveh was one of the oldest cities of civilization dating back to before 4000 B.C. The ancient city is located around 230 miles west of the Iraqi city of Baghdad on the Tigris River.

During Jonah's day the walled portion of the city would have made about an eight-mile circumference. When considering the area outside the walls, the city and its surrounding suburbs could have been as many as sixty miles in circumference. It was a huge city to say the least. After receiving his commission from God, Jonah decides to flee in the opposite direction to Tarshish. Located in southern Spain, Tarshish was a small Phoenician colony on the edge of civilization. Twice in verse three we read that Jonah's purpose for the trip to Tarshish was to *flee from the presence of the Lord.* Could it be that Jonah wished to resign from his job as prophet of the Lord? He no longer wanted to be a messenger of God.

The great storm

As soon as Jonah boards the ship headed west, he settles down in the lowest cabin of the ship and goes to sleep. After the boat gets out to sea, God causes a great storm to come up with fierce winds that rock the ship violently. The ship was battered to the point that it was about to be broken up. The ship hands begin to throw off unnecessary items and pray to their gods. As they are running through the cargo hold looking for anything to lighten the ship, they come upon Jonah sleeping. He is rebuked by the captain and is told to get up and call on his God for deliverance from the storm. As it becomes evident that the prayers to the idols are not working, the shipmen determined that there must be someone on board responsible for the great storm. They cast lots and it fell upon Jonah. Only when the lot fell upon him, and they began to ask questions did Jonah confess.

Jonah tells the sea goers that he was a Hebrew and worshiped the Lord, the creator of all. He told them that he was fleeing from the presence of the Lord. *How could you do this*, the pagan men asked. What a rebuke to the prophet of the Lord who had needlessly put the lives of these innocent men in danger. While this conversation is going on, the sea is becoming increasingly boisterous. Jonah asks to be thrown overboard so that the sea will be calm, and the lives of the sailors be spared. At first, they ignore his request and row feverishly against the wind. But their efforts were in vain, and finally they pray to God asking that they not perish in the storm and that they not be held accountable for innocent blood in throwing Jonah overboard. In their prayer they also confess the right of God to do as He pleases, and it seems that they now believed in God. Verse sixteen says, *Then the men feared the Lord greatly, and they offered a sacrifice to the Lord and made vows.* After throwing Jonah into the sea, the sea stopped its raging, 1:15.

Jonah and the great fish

Chapter one concludes by telling the reading audience that God appointed a great fish to swallow Jonah. Jonah spent three days and three nights inside the fish. The miracle is not that God prepared a fish to swallow Jonah… it is that Jonah survived for three days and nights inside the great animal. There are several large fish that are capable of completely swallowing a man. Sperm whales, great white sharks, or Rhinodon sharks have been suggested as possibilities for the type of fish God could have used to carry out His purpose. But let us be careful lest we spend so much time on the episode with the great fish that we lose sight of the other important messages found within this book.

If it can be said that Jonah ran away from God in chapter one, it can easily be said that he ran toward God in chapter two. If Jonah was to be saved from this situation, help was going to have to come from God. Chapter 2:2 says that Jonah cried out from the depth of Sheol. In Hebrew, Sheol refers to the realm of the dead. Jonah probably felt as if he was as good as dead at this point—knowing his only escape would be because of the grace and mercy of God. His prayer in the opening verses of chapter two is one of thanksgiving and praise. He acknowledges that being thrown overboard and washed around in the sea was part of God's discipline on him. Yet even in his despair, he hopes to *look again toward Your [God's] holy temple,* 2:4.

Verse five gives us just a little insight into the cramped, uncomfortable conditions found inside the great fish. Water was all around him; he found himself gasping for air and had weeds wrapped around his head. Add to this the smell of decaying food the great fish had eaten, being unable to move, and knowing that all the while he is descending deeper and deeper into the ocean. As Jonah began to lose consciousness, he remembered God and prayed. He thanks God that his prayers reached heaven and that God listened to him. In verses eight and nine Jonah promises to sacrifice to God and fulfill the vows he had made.

The Sailor's Changing Perspective in Jonah 1

REFERENCE	OBSERVATIONS
Jonah 1:5	*sailors become afraid*
Jonah 1:10	*the men became extremely frightened*
Jonah 1:14	*they called upon the Lord*
Jonah 1:16	*they feared the Lord greatly; offered sacrifices/vows*

The chapter concludes with God responding to Jonah's prayer by commanding the great fish to vomit Jonah onto dry land. Scripture is silent as to how exactly God spoke to the fish or where Jonah was deposited. How long did it take Jonah to return to Israel? Did he bypass Israel and head directly to Nineveh? These are questions without answers.

Applications for Today

Who can flee from the presence of God?

This may be the most significant lesson from these two chapters. The Hebrew writer has said, *there is no creature hidden from His sight, but all things are open and laid bare to the eyes of Him with whom we have to do,* Hebrews 4:13. Running from Him is fruitless. There is nowhere we can go to escape His presence. Even in the depths of the sea, buried in the belly of the great fish, God heard and answered the prayer of Jonah. Each man will stand before God and give an account for the deeds done in the body, 2 Corinthians 5:9-10. *...It is appointed for men to die once and after this comes the judgment,* Hebrews 9:27. See also Psalm139:7-10.

The submission of the heathen sailors to God stands in great contrast to Jonah's prideful refusal to yield to God's will.

As you read through Jonah 1 with the entire episode of the storm, there is a great contrast between the humble attitudes of the sailors and Jonah's stubborn refusal to submit to God. In fact, their fear is transformed from just fearing a storm to fearing the Almighty God. Note verse five: *the soldiers became afraid.* In verse ten the intensity is much greater: *the men became extremely frightened.* This is after they realize which deity Jonah served. Jonah served the Lord. As they are fighting against the wind, trying desperately to steer the ship back to land, their prayers are now directed to the Lord, 1:14. And by verse sixteen we are told *the men feared the LORD greatly.* Contrast this to Jonah's sleeping in the cargo hold of the ship during the midst of the storm. His mind is not on God. The captain of the ship rebukes Jonah, *How is it that you are sleeping?* Later, when the shipmen realize which God Jonah served, they ask, how could you do this? This is another sharp rebuke to the prophet.

Everyone needs to hear God's message of repentance and deliverance

Jonah was extremely nationalistic. The last thing he wanted to do was to go to the capitol city of Israel's greatest enemy and inform them of an opportunity to repent. Such a cruel and violent people only deserved the judgment of God, he must have thought. Yet, his responsibility was simply to relay the message. So is ours. If those who hear God's teaching repent, we need to praise God. If they do not, we need to pray for their repentance— because eternity in hell is not desirous for any person.

Sometimes people must go to the lowest depths to realize their dependence upon God.

Jonah literally went to the lowest depths before he realized his need for God. It took his being driven to the point of physical death before his will was broken. The prayer from inside the fish is one of repentance. It is one where he vows to fulfill the will of God. The prodigal son in Luke 15 had to reach the same point before he came to his senses. A person does not have to go to this level if he will only soften his heart. How soft and pliable is your heart?

For discussion

1. Where did Jonah call home? In what time did he live?

2. Describe the social, political, and economic times of Jonah.

3. Talk about the state of the Assyrian nation during the eighth century B.C.

4. Would you describe Assyria as kind and compassionate or as a brutal and cruel nation? Why?

5. What are the two main messages from Jonah?

6. What was Jonah's purpose in fleeing to Tarshish? Where is Tarshish?

7. Read Chapter 1. There are three miracles within the text. Find them and list them below.

8. Would you describe Jonah's prayer as a prayer of thanksgiving or repentance or both?

9. Describe Jonah's experience inside the great fish.

10. How can we become more aware that we can never escape being in the presence of God?

11. Describe the progression of the faith of the sailors as you go throughout chapter one.

12. How are Jonah and the prodigal son alike?

Jonah 3-4: Jonah Preaches to Nineveh

Introduction

IN OUR PREVIOUS LESSON we discussed Jonah's refusal to go to Nineveh and his adventurous ride at sea. After Jonah returns to dry land, some wonder if he goes back to his hometown of Gath-hepher where God comes to him a second time calling him to go to Nineveh. Wherever he went after the sea creature episode, God found Jonah and expected him to fulfill his mission. And so, he goes. We are told that Nineveh was an extremely large city. Most historians suggest that during Jonah's time the circumference of Nineveh would have been around eight miles. When factoring in the suburbs and surrounding areas, Nineveh would increase to a sixty-mile circumference. The term three days walk in verse three probably means that it took Jonah three days to deliver the message to the city. Imagine him going to street corners, public gathering places, temples, etc. issuing the warning, *yet forty days and Nineveh will be overthrown.* "Overthrown" as used here would have been understood by the people as complete destruction.

Why forty days some have asked? This would have been a period where God waited to see how the people responded to Jonah's message. If by the end of the forty days they failed to respond, God would destroy the city. This is not the first conditional time where God held out for the repentance of man. Before the flood, God gave mankind one hundred and twenty years to repent, Genesis 6:3. God gave Israel innumerable opportunities to repent, and when they failed to do so, they suffered punishment from God. In Scripture the term forty has a special significance as it is "considered the number of probations, testing, punishment, chastisement and humiliation."[3] Consider:

- Genesis 7:12 — God sent forty days of rain to flood the earth.
- Exodus 16:35 — Israel spent forty years in the wilderness after the majority rejected God.
- Exodus 24:18 — Moses spent forty days on Mount Sinai receiving the law.
- Matthew 4:2 — Jesus spent forty days in the wilderness being tempted by Satan.
- A period of around forty years elapsed between the establishment of the church and the destruction of Jerusalem in 70 A.D.

Nineveh's response

The simple message Jonah delivered had an extreme impact, reaching as far as the king. His words penetrated the entire city, from the greatest to the least of people. Luke 11:30 says, ...*Jonah became a sign to the Ninevites.* Perhaps the story of the storm at sea, Jonah's predicament inside the great fish, and his deliverance preceded him to Nineveh? Could his physical appearance have changed because of spending three days and nights being churned inside a fish? Whatever the case, Jonah's message worked on the hearts of his listeners. When word reached the king, he proclaimed a fast, ordering that neither man nor beast eat anything. How long this fast lasted we are not told. You may remember from a previous lesson that fasting during Old Testament times was a sign of grief and anguish. It was an effort to move God so that He would relent of His impending punishment. The King urged everyone to cease from their wicked ways and *the violence, which is in his hands,* 3:8. Here is a pagan king who recognized the evil in his own city and set the example by humbling himself to God to stave off destruction. Verse nine is important in that it shows how the king recognized the sovereignty of God. *Who knows, God may turn and relent and withdraw His burning anger...* He recognized that God did not have to issue repentance, but if He did, it would solely be by His grace and mercy.

Verse ten states the fact of Nineveh's repentance and that it led to a reversal by God concerning the destruction of the city. Their repentance was genuine. They did deeds of repentance and *turned from their wicked way.* With God's relenting of punishment, it shows us His deep care and concern for all men. He wishes to dispense His grace and mercy on all men, including the most wicked and cruel. What a lesson for each one of us to learn! How long did Nineveh's repentance and good deeds last? We are not told.

Secular history tells us that during and after the reign of Adad-nirari III (810-783 B.C.) Assyria made a move toward monotheism. Some attribute this to the preaching of Jonah, but that is nothing more than speculation. We do know in the generations after Jonah that Assyria returned to its wicked ways, becoming even more wicked and violent than before. They would conquer the northern ten tribes of Israel after a three-year siege in 722 B.C. Eventually this powerful nation would fade into history, being absorbed by the great Babylonian Empire in 612 B.C.

Jonah's reaction to the events in Nineveh

Jonah becomes extremely displeased at the repentance of a people he loved to hate. He felt the Ninevites deserved punishment and was sad to see God relent from the calamity He was going to bring upon them. Jonah 4:2 gives us the real reason why Jonah attempted to flee to Tarshish in chapter one. He feared God would spare them. This is in great contrast to his thanksgiving for God's grace and mercy in delivering him from the *depth* of Sheol in chapter two. Jonah knew well the character of God, and while he wanted those blessings for himself, he absolutely did not want those blessings extended on a people whom he felt unworthy. He was so disgusted with the repentance of the Ninevites that he wished he could die, 4:3. There has been much speculation on the reasons why Jonah could have been angry with the result of what most prophets and preachers would call successful preaching. Some of the theories include:

- Damage to his reputation as a prophet. He prophesied doom on the people, but they repented, and God relented from punishment. It would appear to others that something he prophesied did not occur.
- If Nineveh repented, this heightened the possibility of their remaining in power long enough to encroach upon and eventually take over the Israelite nation.
- Simple prejudice against the Assyrians.
- Assuming the best, Jonah might have possessed a desire to use Nineveh as an example of God's punishment of sin to persuade Israel to return from its own sinful conduct.

Whatever the basis for his anger, he was not justified to act in the way he did.

God's response

Some suggest that once again God demonstrates extreme grace and mercy for the way He responds to Jonah's "temper-tantrum." After Jonah wishes for death, God asks, *do you have good reason to be angry?* As a father would to his child, God seeks to make Jonah stop and think about his anger. God wanted Jonah to think for himself and adjust his attitude. God's reaction here is another demonstration of his patience and longsuffering. This is the second time that God has had to teach the prophet a lesson. Verse four does not tell how Jonah responded to God's question. From here Jonah moves eastward into the desert and sits down to see what will become of Nineveh.

We might speculate that this was still during the forty-day grace period he spoke of in chapter three. It has been suggested that he figured and/or hoped Nineveh's repentance would not last forty days. In the desert Jonah prepared himself a shelter to shade himself from the extreme heat and sat down to wait. As Jonah is holding out in the desert, God caused a plant to grow up over Jonah to give him shade from the intense heat of the desert. He was comforted from the heat and very thankful for the plant. Overnight, God prepared a worm to come eat the plant. It died. On the next day God sent a brutal east wind, which together with the burning hot sun, made Jonah so miserable he wished he would die.

God comes to Jonah again in verse nine and asks, *do you have good reason to be angry about the plant?* Jonah's response suggests total exasperation. He says, *I have good reason to be angry, even to death.* To this God responds, *you had compassion on the plant for which you did not work and which you did not cause to grow, which came up overnight and perished overnight.* Here is Jonah, so upset over the destruction of a plant yet so indifferent, unconcerned, and even hopeful for hundreds of thousands of deaths in Nineveh. On this Hailey has written, "Man can become greatly concerned and disturbed when that which directly affects him is touched by the finger of providence; but he can be utterly indifferent, even hard, to that which may be of infinitely greater value when this does not affect him."[4]

Jonah's concern for the plant was only for his own self-interests, not for love. He did not have a connection to the gourd (he didn't plant it), and yet he was sorry for its demise. Contrast that to God's love, care, and concern for His creation. Even though the Ninevites were a very wicked people, God still cared for them. Verse eleven tells us that God held out for Nineveh's repentance because of over one hundred and twenty thousand persons who could not distinguish between their right and left hand. Most take this to mean that these were children. God felt it necessary to give them a chance to grow up and make the choice to serve Him. Not only were the people precious in the sight of God, but livestock and animals were also something important to Him. Indeed, God loves all His creation.

What became of Jonah after this little book abruptly ends? No one knows. Did he repent? Did he continue sulking? Smith speculates that "Jonah could have intended this account, which puts himself in such a bad light, to be a confession. If that is true, then Jonah straightened out his thinking."[5] Whatever happened to Jonah, this little book is one that today's reader can profit greatly from.

Lessons for Today

God lives for second chances

Chapter three opens with the following line: *the word of the Lord came to Jonah the second time …* Did not God have the right to be finished with Jonah after his outright rebellion in boarding the ship to Tarshish? Yet God sought to use the experience as a lesson to help Jonah come to a better realization of God's salvation and grace. How many would argue that God would have the right to be finished with Jonah after his temper tantrum in chapter four? But if he repented, God would have welcomed Jonah back into His grace. How wonderful it is to serve the God we do! Indeed, *God is a gracious and compassionate God, slow to anger and abundant in lovingkindness, and one who relents concerning calamity.* Are the characteristics of God not testimony to his holding out for our repentance? See 2 Peter 3:9-11.

God holds out for the repentance of all people—no matter how evil they are

It has been well documented as to the brutality and cruelty of the Assyrians. Even the king recognized the great wickedness and violence of his people. If they would repent, God would cease his plans of bringing destruction to Nineveh. This is a lesson we need to learn. We can be more susceptible to our own prejudices and biases than we care to admit. One of Jonah's greatest problems seems to be that he felt the Ninevites were not worthy of God's salvation. His reason for going to the desert east of the city was that he was hoping to see them destroyed. He would have relished in their destruction.

Scripture is full of exhortations for us to watch out for a superior disposition that looks down on others. An entire chapter in Luke is devoted to Jesus' teaching on this matter. Luke fifteen and part of sixteen give us rich teaching on everyone's need for forgiveness, and these chapters challenge us to be forgiving and accepting of those whom God has forgiven.

God uses extreme patience and longsuffering in dealing with our attitudes

Place yourself in God's shoes in Jonah 4:4. Would you have answered the testy and arrogant prophet in this way? God is holding out that his question will prompt Jonah to think about his attitude and conduct. We can easily see Jonah's shortcomings, but it can be very hard to see our own attitude problems. We need to praise God that He has been so patient and longsuffering with us when our behavior and conduct might have paralleled Jonah's.

God has power over all aspects of His creation

In chapter one we learn that God has power over the forces of weather. Not only did He create the wind that began the storm, but He had the power to calm the storm once Jonah was cast overboard. In chapter two we learn that God has control over the sea creatures as He prepared the fish that swallowed Jonah. After Jonah repents, God directs the fish to vomit Jonah out on dry land. In chapter four God reveals His power over the plants and small animals of the earth. All His creation is under His control and can be used to further His purposes and will.

It is ironic that a heathen and extremely wicked people repented at their first opportunity, yet Israel failed to repent after relentless pleading by God through the prophets

Israel had all the blessings of being with God. They witnessed God's signs, miracles, and wonders. They had been a constant recipient of God's marvelous blessings. All of this seemed to make them feel secure, smug, and self-important. When they fell into sin, Israel often had to fall to the lowest depths to realize their dependence upon God. Yet when a prophet of the Lord came to Nineveh, the people were humble enough to recognize the power of God and the sureness of the calamity which would fall upon them for any lack of repentance. Nineveh's zealousness to repent, from the top to bottom of society, was a sure "slap-in-the-face" to the Israelites who had every opportunity to obey.

For discussion

1. How large was Nineveh during the lifetime of Jonah?

2. Explain the symbolism behind the period of forty days in scripture.

3. What kind of reaction did Nineveh have to Jonah's preaching?

4. Describe the attitude of the king of Nineveh when he heard of the need to repent. Are there any lessons we can take from this? If so, what?

5. What in Jonah 3:10 signals true repentance from the Ninevites?

6. What was Jonah's real reason for going to Tarshish in chapter one? See 4:2.

7. Do you think Jonah was praising the attributes of God in 4:2?

8. What are some speculations on the reasons for Jonah's anger?

9. Read 4:4. Would you have been as patient with Jonah as God was? What does this teach us about God?

10. What was the intent of God's lesson to Jonah in 4:6-11?

11. What are some important lessons we can learn from this section of Jonah?

Amos 1-3:
God Will Judge the Nations

Introduction

THE MINISTRY OF AMOS took place during the very prosperous and peaceful eighth century B.C. Amos hailed from the rural town of Tekoa, some ten to twelve miles south of Jerusalem. Sitting in very rugged hill country, Tekoa's elevation of 2500 feet allowed it to have sweeping views of the Jordan River Valley and the wilderness surrounding the Dead Sea. "Amos" comes from a Hebrew word meaning "burden bearer." Some believe "Amos" is an abbreviated form of the name *Amasiah* which means "born by the LORD."

In our modern terminology we might liken Amos to a rancher. Verse 1 tells us he raised sheep. Amos 7:14 tells us he was a herdsman, and a *grower of sycamore figs.* Hailey suggests that Amos could have raised a small, rugged type of sheep called "nakads." The wool from these sheep would have been of great quality and very valuable. Sycamore figs were often grown in the wilderness near the Dead Sea. Sycamore figs were usually eaten by those in the lower strata of society and had to be pinched or bruised before it would ripen. Amos seems to be a man of means, educated, and someone aware of the world events of his time. He held nothing back in informing Israel of God's message. In speaking of himself he says:

> I am not a prophet, nor am I the son of a prophet; for I am a herdsman and a grower of sycamore figs. But the Lord took me from following the flock and the Lord said to me, Go prophesy to My people Israel, 7:14-15.

From this Amos appears as a man who would have been well suited to address the life of excess and ease enjoyed by the citizens of Israel.

The ministry of Amos would have been in the years between 792-740 B.C. In 1:1, we are told that his ministry began two years before the earthquake. Tradition says this earthquake occurred when Uzziah attempted to perform the duties of the priests, 2 Chronicles 26:16. Uzziah was struck with leprosy as his punishment from God. If this tradition is true, then we can infer that Amos' ministry in the north began around 752 B.C. Some guess that he could have spent as much as two years preaching in Israel until he was asked to go back to Judah by Amaziah, the priest of Bethel, 7:12-13. Could chapters 8-9 have been written after Amos' return to Judah?

It is interesting to consider that God would choose a man from Judah to travel to his kinsman in the north to preach to Israel. He would have been seen as an outsider while proclaiming God's message throughout the country. His message is very objective and sends forth a message of justice.

The World of Amos

TIME	ISRAEL		JUDAH	
	KING	PROPHET	KING	PROPHET
760		JONAH (780-760)		
	JEROBOAM II (793-753)		UZZIAH (792-740)	
750		AMOS (760-750)		
	MENAHEM (752-742)	*Zechariah ruled for 8 months in 753. Assassinated by Shallum who ruled for 1 month in 752. Shalom assassinated by Menahem.		
740	PEKAH (742-732)	*Pekahiah ruled from 742-740.	JOTHAM (750-732) *Jotham was co-regent with Uzziah for 10 years.	ISAIAH (762-690)
730		HOSEA (750-725)		
	HOSHEA (732-722)		AHAZ (JEHOSOPHAT) (735-716)	
720				MICAH (735-700)
710	Northern Kingdom Destroyed by Assyria			
700	722 BC		HEZEKIAH (716-687)	

The world of Amos

Amos prophesied during the days of King Uzziah of Judah and Jeroboam II in Israel. These were "good" times politically. Assyria was inwardly focused with weak kings, internal rebellion, and strife. Both Israel and Judah expanded the borders of their kingdom and their military power. Uzziah and Jeroboam II were strong leaders and helped their nations prosper into heights not seen since the days of the United Kingdom. Until the arrival of Tiglath-Pileser on the throne of Assyria in 745 B.C., God's people enjoyed relative peace on all sides. After this, Assyria would begin a rapid expansion to the west, culminating in the fall of the northern ten tribes in 722 B.C. Internally, the politicians of the day were corrupt. In 3:9-10 we read: Proclaim on the citadels in Ashdod and on the citadels in the land of Egypt and say, "assemble yourselves on the mountains of Samaria and see the great tumults within her and the oppressions in her midst. But they do not know how to do what is right," declares the LORD, "these who hoard up violence and devastation in their citadels." Political leaders used violence and oppression to further themselves and did not serve as advocates for the poor. Amos 5:10 tells us that the leaders disliked the judges that upheld righteousness. This says a great deal about the character of the people during this time.

The economic times of Amos' day were very rich and prosperous. Amos addresses the problems associated with a rich and affluent society.

- 3:11 — many of the people dwelt in rich palaces.
- 3:12 — the people slept on couches and "silk cushions." (ASV)
- 3:15 — some people had winter and summer homes.
- 4:1-3 — when women wanted a feast, they did not care how it happened, even if it crushed those who were needy.
- 6:1-7 — the people were at ease, sleeping on beds of ivory and listened to fine music, etc.

The moral and religious conditions were no better. Perhaps this passage sums it up best:

> Thus says the LORD, for three transgressions of Israel and for four I will not revoke its punishment, Because they sell the righteous for money And the needy for a pair of sandals. These who pant after the very dust of the earth on the head of the helpless Also turn aside the way of the humble; And a man and his father resort to the same girl In order to profane My holy name. On garments taken as pledges they stretch out beside every altar, And in the house of their God they drink the wine of those who have been fined, 2.6-8.

Amos 5:11 speaks of the extortion of the poor by the rich. Because of their actions, God would bring strong judgment against them.

The Lord roars from Zion

Verse one tells us that Amos received his prophetic message in a vision. This message came from the Lord and was directed primarily at the northern ten tribes, Israel. Verse two parallels Joel 3:16 (*the LORD roars from Zion*) and from this Amos begins to speak of the sudden and swift judgment that is about to come upon Israel and its neighbors.

Verse two also identifies the dwelling place of Jehovah: Zion, *from Jerusalem He utters His voice*. This would have been an indictment on the northern tribes who had long forsaken Jerusalem as the place of their worship, serving God from altars in Dan and Bethel. Zion was looked upon by the people as the dwelling place of God, and the roar of His voice would signify judgment on the entire land.

Amos 1:3-2:3 contain judgments against six nations surrounding Israel and Judah. These nations' iniquity had risen to the level where justice could no longer ignore it. God was about to punish them for the great evil they had committed. All nations, not just Israel and Judah, were accountable to God. Evil will not go unpunished. It is interesting to note a repetitive phrase found in announcing doom on each nation. In identifying Damascus as a target of God's justice, Amos says, *for three transgressions of Damascus and for four I will not revoke its punishment,* 1:3. The same words are used in addressing each nation mentioned in the first two chapters, including Israel and Judah. The phrase was common in writing during this time (see Proverbs 30:15) and suggests a cumulative effect. The wickedness of these nations was growing year by year and God could no longer tolerate it. God says each time that He would not revoke its punishment.

Judgment on Damascus, 1:3-5

Damascus was the capital of Syria, located to the north of Jerusalem. Damascus played a key role in the politics of the entire region and was the power most threatening to Israel's security. They would be punished for their war atrocities. 2 Kings 8:7-15 and 13:7 gives us the historical account of the dominance of Aram (Syria) over Israel. The thresher mentioned in Amos 1:3 was probably a drag of heavy wooden timbers with sharp stones or iron points attached on the bottom. As the horse pulled the drag, the driver stood on top of the timbers adding weight to press the stones and/or iron into the ground. Prisoners would be lined up on the ground and then soldiers would drive the thresher over the prisoners.

The house of Hazael and cities of Ben-Hadad were to be destroyed by God. Hazael, king of Aram from 843-796 B.C., caused great problems for three successive kings of Israel. Jehoahaz finally defeated and killed Ben-Hadad III, Hazael's son (796-770 B.C.). Historical references to Hazael and Ben-Hadad III are seen in 2 Kings 8-10 and 13. The people of Aram would be exiled to Kir. Kir means *a walled place* and its exact location is unknown. Most people speculate that the people of Aram would be sent as captives to the land from which they came, north and east of Israel.

Judgment on Gaza, 1:6-8

Gaza was in Philistia, southwest of Jerusalem. Gaza, Ashdod, Ashkelon, and Eklon represent the entirety of Philistine society, which was long known for its participation in the slave trade. They had taken an entire population and delivered it as slaves to Edom. The Edomites would have sold the captive people to traders from around the world. There was no concern for the breaking up of families and their welfare. God would send His judgment on Philistia, and they would lose their identity as a nation, 1:7-8.

Judgment on Tyre, 1:9-10

Tyre was located to the north of Israel and was a major seaport on the Mediterranean. Like the Philistines, God condemns the people for delivering up an entire population to Edom, 1:9. Most likely the people they delivered to Edom were Israelites and for this they were held accountable to violating the covenant of brotherhood. Centuries before, there had been a peace treaty signed between Hiram, King of Tyre and David, King of Israel. God expects people (and nations) to live up to their word. For their treachery they would be destroyed. During the sixth century B.C., Nebuchadnezzar took up the task of destroying Tyre. The city would be destroyed by Alexander the Great centuries later.

Judgment on Edom, 1:11-12

The Edomites were descendants of Esau, the brother of Jacob. Residing to the south of the Dead Sea, Edom was located on important trade routes leading to the east. Much of the nation's income came through the profit of the slave trade. Edom had long been an enemy of the Israelites, and in this place God calls out their continual hatred toward Israel. Parts of verse eleven parallel with Obadiah 10-12. Teman and Bozrah were principal cities of Edom. Because of their lack of compassion and love, Edom would be destroyed.

Judgment on Ammon, 1:13-15

Ammon was located northeast of the Dead Sea on the edge of the Arabian Desert. Both Ammon and Moab were descendants of Lot, Genesis 19:37-38. They were guilty of unimaginable atrocities against the children of Israel to expand the borders of their kingdom. They heaped out torture on even the unborn, ripping open the wombs of mothers. Some have speculated this was done to decrease the male descendants of Israel. Rabbah was the chief city of the Ammonites, and Amos prophesies that it will be destroyed with divine vengeance, and the king and ruling families would be carried off into captivity.

Judgment on Moab, 2:1-3

Moab is mentioned next in Amos' prophecy. Some feel it is listed directly after Ammon because of their ancestral heritage. In this passage Moab is condemned for committing what might have been considered the utmost form of disrespect in the ancient world: exhuming the dead body and burning the bones of the king of Edom. Hubbard writes, "Burning a body was an extreme form of criminal punishment designed to purge completely the land of its wickedness." [1] Some commentators feel that the Moabites would have used the ashes of the king of Edom in the erection of a building where one of their gods would have been worshipped. For this, God would send fire down on the Moabites. Isaiah and Jeremiah would also comment on the severity of God's judgment against Moab. See Isaiah 15:5; 16:11; and Jeremiah 48:36.

Judgment on Judah, 2:4-5

The six nations discussed heretofore are all in the same region as the people of God. Now the focus comes home to Judah and Israel. They too had done great wickedness in the sight of God. Judah's wickedness was in the form of religious apostasy. Their crime was against the Lord. They *rejected the law of the **Lord** And have not kept His statutes*, 2:4. They delighted in idolatry and the wisdom of men. Even prophets, several good kings (Hezekiah, etc.), and priests could not turn the people back to God's way. This ultimately led them to destruction in 587 B.C. by Nebuchadnezzar.

Judgment on Israel, 2:6-16

While the sins of Judah were primarily spiritual in nature, the sins of their northern neighbors were that of a moral and political nature. The indictment begins in verses six through eight as Amos points out Israel's covetousness, immorality, and lack of compassion for the poor. Selling the poor into slavery (2:6) indicates the character of a people who had long forsaken God. Israel's society during the days of Amos was very litigious, which resulted in the trampling on the head of the helpless. Many Israelite landowners had an insatiable desire to acquire more land.

Going along with this was the rampant immorality. This would have related to the worship of Baal. Men and their sons would have thought nothing in using the same prostitute—all in the name of religion. Verse eight mentions garments taken as pledges. These were the outer garments worn by the poor, and if they were pawned, they were to be returned by dusk, Exodus 22:26; Deuteronomy 24:12. This law was being violated, and again, it reveals the character of the people of Israel. This corruption and immorality involved the entirety of society—even those in the ruling class. While all this immorality was going on, persons were in the temple hypocritically praising God.

After outlining these sins, Amos contrasts the great acts of God in taking care of His chosen people. God gave them their land, delivering it to Israel from the Amorites. God had taken a strong and powerful enemy and delivered it into the hands of Israel for victory. God was the one who brought them out of Egypt, sustaining them through the wilderness. God had liberated them and blessed them. God made Himself available to prophets so His message could be communicated to the people. Nazarites were people who had consecrated their lives in service to God. They were to abstain from the consumption of grapes and any of its products. They were not to shave their head (see Numbers 6). They were a symbol of being made separate for the Lord, but Israel had forced the Nazarites to violate their vows. They prohibited the prophets from prophesying. Rejection of all that God did for them reveals the ultimate in ingratitude.

Because of their rebellion and lack of thankfulness, in verses thirteen through sixteen God reveals what He is going to do to Israel. The weight of God's judgment would come crashing down upon them. The enemy would come and:

> Flight will perish from the swift, And the stalwart will not strengthen his power, Nor the mighty man save his life. He who grasps the bow will not stand his ground, The swift of foot will not escape, Nor will he who rides the horse save his life. Even the bravest among the warriors will flee naked in that day, declares the Lord, 2:14-16.

There was a day of the Lord coming for Israel. They would not go unpunished.

Amos defends his right to speak, 3:1-8

God was bringing judgment against Israel. The relationship between God and Israel was special and is brought out by the usage of family in verse one. They were privileged: *you only I have chosen among all the families of the earth*, 3:2. God had redeemed Israel from bondage and had made a covenant with them. Because of their refusal to keep this covenant, they would be punished. The language of verse two suggests that God knew Israel in a very personal way, which was more special than the relationships with other nations. Israel had been called to a higher plane and because of their violation of the covenant, God would punish them for all their iniquities. In verses three through eight Amos defends his right to speak. He had been sent out on a mission to deliver God's message to Israel. Israel needed to know they had crossed the line and would be caught in their sin just as a lion roars when it catches its prey and just like a bird caught in a trap. God's message should have made the people move in fear. They needed to be aware of the impending doom coming on their nation.

Judgment is coming, 3:9-15

Israel took great comfort in that they were God's chosen people. They felt safe and secure to engage in whatever conduct they pleased without punishment. The message of Amos and other prophets is that God was going to hold them responsible for violating the covenant they made with God at Mount Sinai. Divine favor had now become a thing of the past. Israel would be destroyed. Their great enemy (Assyria) would surround the land, rob the nation of its strength, and loot its cities. Samaria (Israel's capitol) would be destroyed.

Imagine how this message must have sounded to a materialistic, arrogant, and prosperous society. No doubt Amos' message fell on many deaf ears who could not possibly imagine their land being destroyed. Living in the lap of luxury (3:14-15), persons living in the Northern Kingdom would be brought down and destroyed by their great enemy, the Assyrians.

For discussion

1. Where was the home of Amos? What was his occupation before becoming a prophet?

2. Describe the political times of Amos.

3. Describe the social & economic times of Amos.

4. Why do you think God would choose a herdsman from Judah to bear His message to the northern tribes?

5. What does the phrase for three transgressions of _____ and four mean?

6. Who were Hazael and Ben-Hadad III?

7. What was the sin that connected Gaza, Tyre, and Edom? What made this sin so devastating?

8. What was the atrocity committed by Ammon?

9. Why did God bring swift and severe judgment on Moab?

10. What was the nature of Judah's sin?

11. Find four separate sins committed by Israel in 2:6-8.

12. Describe the ways God showed His favor on Israel in 2:9-12.

13. How severe was God's judgment going to be? See 2:13-16.

14. How is God's relationship with Israel described in Chapter 3?

15. How did arrogance, prosperity, and materialism lead to Israel's downfall?

Amos 4-6:
Condemnation for Israel

Introduction

IN THE PREVIOUS THREE CHAPTERS Amos begins the book by a stinging prophecy against the neighbors of Israel and Judah. Then God's people are warned of His dissatisfaction with them. Amos was sent to bring a message to the northern ten tribes and by the middle part of chapter two they are clearly in focus. Israel needed to be aware of coming judgment. They were going to fall from rich prosperity to being subjugated as captives to an aggressive nation that would pull down their strength and loot their citadels, 3:11.

Israel's constant refusal to come back to God

The condemnation of Israel continues into chapters four through six. Chapters four and five do seem to offer one last glimmer of hope of being spared from certain destruction: repent on God's terms. What we have in Amos seems to be God's last appeal to His people, hoping against all hope that they will turn to Him, but all the while knowing they will not. Cows of Bashan in Amos 4:1 was directed to the women of Israel and obviously was not a flattering term. These are the wives of the influential upper class in Samaria. They joined with their husbands in oppressing the poor and crushing the needy. Their interests were focused on their own pleasure and enjoyment of life, drawing their husbands in to spend more time banqueting and reveling. God says that the women of Israel will face certain judgment. They will be humbled. Being led away with meat hooks and fishhooks could refer to the Assyrian practice of piercing the lower lip of their captives with a ring. A rope would be attached to this ring and a person would be led off under complete control of their master. They would be led out of the city in single file through the holes in the city wall pierced through by the intruders. They would be completely humbled.

Verses four and five in chapter four point to the religious corruption in Israel. Hailey comments, "there was an abundance of 'religion' in the land, but no true piety and devotion to God."[1] All of what went on in their religion pleased them, but not God. Bethel (4:4) was one of the original places for worship set up by Jeroboam I (931-910 B.C.). Jeroboam did not want his people returning to Jerusalem (in the southern kingdom) to worship God, so golden calves and altars were erected at Dan and Bethel, 1 Kings 12:28-29. Gilgal (4:4) was the first camping spot of Israel after their arrival in the promised land. Most likely, calf worshippers had erected an altar and shrine in this place.

Remember, the only place God commanded His people to worship was in the temple in Jerusalem. Anything else would have been unpleasing in the sight of God. Not only is the place of their worship condemned, but the acts and motives behind their worship are brought to light. While bringing sacrifices, paying tithes, and having freewill offerings were part of the Old Testament law, the motives behind the worship were not pure, making their actions unprofitable. Using leavened bread in worship was condemned under the old law, Leviticus 2:11. Their freewill offerings were made in such a way to draw attention to the amount given and were done without any recognition of the sacredness of worshipping their Creator. This worship was all about them and nothing about God. Verse five goes a long way in showing the condition of their heart: *For so you love to do, you sons of Israel, Declares the Lord God.*

God's Efforts to Move Israel to Repentance

REFERENCE	DESCRIPTION
Amos 4:6	*cleanness of teeth and lack of bread*
Amos 4:7	*withheld rain 3 months before harvest; sending rain to some areas and not to others*
Amos 4:9	*sent a scorching east wind; mildew; and locusts*
Amos 4:10	*sent plagues and disease*
Amos 4:10	*slew Israel's young men with the sword*
Amos 4:11	*overthrew some cities in Israel*

From verse six through the end of the chapter, we read of five ways God tried to prod Israel back to obedience. His prodding went unheeded. This should have not been a surprise to God's people since they had been forewarned. In Deuteronomy 28-29, Israel was warned of certain and just consequences for a violation of the covenant with God. Israel had become so blinded by sin they failed to realize the punishment they received was the judgment of God. *Cleanness of teeth* indicates a lack of food. Amos goes further saying they had a *lack of bread*. We know there were several famines in the years before Amos. One of them was during the reign of Ahab, 1 Kings 17:12, and another during the reign of Jehoram, 2 Kings 4:38, 8:1. These may or may not have been the famines Amos is reminding the people of, but there is little doubt they could look back on their history and recount these devastating famines that decreased their harvests.

We are also told that God caused droughts to take place during their prime growing seasons, affecting the harvest. This was part of the judgment of God. Certain cities would suffer, while others would be spared, 4:8. Even this would not waken the people from their spiritual slumber. Next, God caused a "scorching wind" to blow. This was a strong east wind off the Arabian Desert which would have dried out their crops, gardens, and tender vegetation. Mildew would have been caused by dampness and very warm temperatures. On top of this God sent out plagues of locusts to devour their crops at various times…all with no reaction from Israel. Next, God sent pestilence and disease to afflict the people like what was commonly experienced by Egypt. Egypt had a reputation for disease, which is noted in Deuteronomy 7:15. This part of God's judgment is a direct fulfillment of the following verses in Deuteronomy:

> The Lord will smite you with the boils of Egypt and with tumors and with the scab and with the itch, from which you cannot be healed, Deuteronomy 28:27.

> He will bring back on you all the diseases of Egypt of which you were afraid, and they will cling to you, Deuteronomy 28:60.

God also allowed Israelite soldiers to fall in battle of which the corpses were allowed to lay on the ground causing an intolerable stench. Finally, God caused the complete overthrow of some of their cities. The remains of their cities were small, insignificant, and worthless. And still, Israel did not return.

Because of their continual rejection of God, He says through Amos: *Because I will do this to you, Prepare to meet your God, O Israel*, 4:12. God was going to bring a terrible and unavoidable judgment on them all. What exactly is this judgment? Amos does not specify. When the judgment came, there would be no escape. But even in these words, it seems as if God is holding out for one last chance in that they will turn to Him.

Seek God

As we move into chapter five, Amos laments over Israel. Doom is coming. God is going to pour out His judgment against the people. They needed to prepare. Israel (the virgin, 5:2) was going to fall and would not rise again. None of her allies would move to save her. As a fully functioning nation wielding political influence, her days were finished. Her cities would be decimated—only a small number of Jews would remain. Everyone and everything would suffer.

In 5:4-6, God offers escape from judgment, urging the nation to repent. They needed to seek the Lord in Jerusalem, not Bethel and Gilgal. In other words, they needed to seek God on His terms, in His ways, and submit to His conditions. There was no hope in deliverance through their golden calves. The cities where these shrines had been built would be destroyed. If they failed to come to God, He would *break forth like a fire* which would *consume with none to quench it*, 5:6.

What was supposed to be right and just had been turned into "bitter" injustice that hurt everyone involved. God would pour out vengeance on those who perverted justice. *Wormwood* stands for evil and wrongdoing. These were the ones who had cast down righteousness as a worthless and unprofitable thing in Israelite society. God, who creates the weather, has power over the stars, and brings a new day everyday would bring certain and swift judgment on the unsuspecting people of the northern kingdom.

Israel's Ungodly Society

REFERENCE	BEHAVIOR TYPE
Amos 5:10	*hatred of reproof and those who speak with integrity*
Amos 5:11	*mistreatment of those less fortunate*
Amos 5:12	*numerous and multiple transgressions*
Amos 5:13	*evil times*

Four serious charges

Over the next few verses, Amos points out more areas of guilt.

Hatred of reproof and those who speak with integrity, 5:10

How much does this speak of their society? How much does this speak of our own? When truth is cast down and trampled upon, serious consequences will follow.

Mistreatment of those less fortunate, 5:11

While taking advantage of the poor at every turn, the rich took every opportunity to increase their riches, building homes of well-hewn stone. Those who made plans to live in them would not have the chance because of the judgment of God.

Numerous transgressions, 5:12

Their sins were great in number.

They lived in evil times, 5:13

The times were so bad that righteousness was constantly oppressed. Those who knew the truth and walked uprightly kept silent because of the times in which they lived. The power held in certain places could have been physically dangerous for them to speak out for truth and righteousness.

Seek good that you may live, 5:14

Israel, in 5:14, is called to turn from its evil ways and seek God. *Hate evil, love good, and establish justice in the gate!* 5:15. This would be a complete reversal of actions for the people, yet God holds out that they will be moved to repentance. For God to be moved away from bringing judgment upon them, they needed to love God, goodness, and righteousness with the same intensity they had loved evil.

Did Amos realize that the calls for repentance were falling on deaf ears? Some believe so because of the usage of the word *therefore* in 5:16. The sound of wailing and mourning would be heard through the streets and hillsides of their country. While they assumed that God was with them, He had long left them. When He passed through, the next time there would be a much different result than they expected. Israel would suffer as it never had before.

Those who were looking forward to a coming day of the Lord to heap up punishment and retribution to their enemies would be surprised to see that the day of the Lord had been reserved for them. It would be a day of sheer terror and darkness. There would be *no brightness in it*. No one would escape this judgment. One calamity upon the other would follow them until they were destroyed, 5:19-20.

Empty and vain worship

Their worship to God was an absolute abomination. So much so that God said, *I hate, I reject your festivals, nor do I delight in your solemn assemblies,* 5:21. God would not accept their burnt offerings, grain offerings, and peace offerings. Their songs were nothing but noise of which God would not listen. Their worship was void because it lacked true devotion to God. Their hearts were far from Him. Jesus would charge the people of His day with the same charges in Matthew 15:9.

God did not want just their worship…He wanted their hearts. If He had their hearts, then justice and righteousness would have characterized the nation. Justice would have been seen in the way they lived their lives outwardly: with godly practices in their personal and social lives.

Righteousness was more "internal" in nature—indicating the desire to engage in godly conduct.

Verses twenty-five through twenty-seven tell us the awful truth: Israel had never given themselves fully to God. Even while worshiping God during the forty years in the wilderness, God's people toyed with idolatry. (See also Ezekiel 20:5-8.) They secretly carried along shrines to their idols and worshiped the "star- god." In the original Hebrew these gods are called Sikkuth and Kiyyun. The names of these gods were known to the people as *Sakkuth* and *Kaiwan*. Note that the spelling of the names of both is changed from "a" to "i" in the text. The names of pagan gods were deliberately misspelled in Hebrew literature to mock the idols and further illustrate their shamefulness. *Sakkuth* and *Kaiwan* were associated with the worship of Moloch, an Ammonite deity. Moloch represented the sun-god and was also known as the god of time. *Kaiwan* is also called *Chiun* in the New King James Version. Amos 5:25-26 is quoted by Stephen in Acts 7:42-43. Here *Chiun* is called *Rompha,* and it has been suggested that these names are interchangeable for the same star-god. While Israel was convinced of the need to turn away from idols (Joshua 24:16-18), they were never fully converted to the Lord as seen here in the writing of Amos.

A warning to apathetic and unconcerned people

As Amos preached, much of his preaching would have fallen on the ears of indifferent people. They could have cared less about impending judgment. Amos' message would have seemed so out of place with those who had it made. The people took great security in their fortresses and military capabilities. Who could possibly withstand them? The leaders of Israel are urged to look at neighboring cities in the countries around them. These neighboring cities were comparable to their own and they would soon be swallowed up by the great Assyrian army (if they were not already).

In 6:3-6, Amos gives us some insight on why his message would have been received with a yawn. The people were too busy reveling to even notice the continual strengthening of their enemy: Assyria. Judgment might be coming, but surely it would not happen during their day. These were people who encouraged violence, engaged in abundant self-indulgence, and focused only on self-gratification. Amos said these would *now go into exile at the head of the exiles, And the sprawlers' banqueting will pass away,* 6:7.

Because of the great arrogance of the Northern Kingdom, God says they will be cast away. Everything the nation took pride in sickened God. It seems that the city of Samaria was in view in verse eight. The Israelites took great pride in their city. During the reign of Jeroboam II, the city walls were strengthened greatly. In some places the walls were as much as thirty feet thick. While Samaria was a formidable fortress, it would take Assyria three years to overthrow the city, God says He would *deliver up the city and all it contains*, 6:8.

Not only would the people suffer death by war, but pestilence would overtake them as well. A graphic picture is painted in verses nine and ten. Large families would perish. Death would hover over the people. Dead bodies would be placed in the outer part of the house where the undertaker could come to carry off the bodies. During a siege, burial of the dead was not possible. This would require their bodies to be cremated. These perilous times would come about at the command of the Lord. Everything would be destroyed. Invaders were coming that would destroy the entire northern kingdom. All the territory gained by Jeroboam II would be swallowed up by the Assyrians and the nation of Israel would be destroyed forever.

Lessons for Today

Women play a key role in determining the morality of a society

Women often serve as a spiritual and moral conscience for men. The importance of their role is undeniable. Usually, as their conduct goes, so goes the nation. The women in Israel during the days of Amos pushed their husbands to engage in acts of unrighteousness and encouraged them to slack off in their responsibilities. This says much about the low level of morality in the country. What of our own? Where are we headed?

Self-centered and carnal worship practices do not please God

A lack of worship was not the problem. Israel had that down to a science. Continual offerings, sacrifices, and rituals were performed, all in the name of God. But these actions were not accepted by God; in fact, they made Him sick and disgusted. Israel had never given their heart to God and after centuries of coaxing, God had finally reached His limit. Considering this there are many lessons for us. While we must worship God *in truth*, we must worship Him *in spirit*, John 4:23-24. We must not concentrate so much on the form of worship that we remove our hearts from our offerings to God. Also, Israel had created a form of worship that was convenient and pleasing to itself. They did not want to worship God in Jerusalem, so they erected shrines in Bethel and Dan. Their corrupted form of worship did not please God in the least. So many today have corrupted worship into a religion of convenience and entertainment. Could God be saying, *Take away from Me the noise of your songs?* (Amos 5:23)

Sin can blind us to the chastisement of God

Throughout chapter four God lists the ways He had tried to prompt Israel to repent and turn back to Him. Deuteronomy 28 and 29 lists certain penalties for violation of the covenant. God explains through Amos that He had brought about these punishments because they were violating the covenant made with Him. While these judgments crippled the nation, they were blinded in that they did not recognize God was trying to tell them something. Sin is blinding and can lead to arrogance. We can be blinded to calls to repentance. Let us beware of the deceptiveness of sin.

God continually holds out for man's repentance

As we read through these chapters, we get the idea that had Israel repented, God would have relented from the certain punishment He was going to bring upon them, even at this late date. But while God hoped for their repentance, for them to *have life* they would need to seek God on His terms and in His place. They could not expect to find God in the golden calves at Bethel and Gilgal. They needed to go to Jerusalem, where God was, and seek Him in the way He wanted. Likewise, we cannot make up our own rules in coming to God. We must go through Jesus and make a full-fledged commitment to serve God. Only in this way will God accept us.

The times of today are very similar to the days of Amos

There is nothing new under the sun. Man is no more sinful today than he ever has been. Sin has just as much a grip on our society as it did during the days of Amos. While we must realize that fact, it is interesting to compare our society with what Amos experienced. Americans have largely become rich, arrogant, and secure. Could our society be *too busy* to listen to and consider God's message? Is God's truth too antiquated and simplistic for our sophisticated society? While we sit in luxurious homes with every modern convenience, have we been *brought near the seat of violence?* Our culture would do well to learn from history. Societies that lose respect for righteousness and truth will ultimately perish.

Apathy can deafen us from the plain and simple teaching of God

We can imagine Amos teaching with power and urgency. Yet it got only a yawn from the people at large. Israel had neglected the great blessings of God and had become self-satisfied and content. There was no need to worry; even if a day of judgment was coming, it would not come in their lifetime, 6:3. This apathy led to their destruction. Throughout Scripture we are warned of the danger of apathy, yet it has a grip on too many Christians. Let us remember the words of the Hebrew writer:

> For this reason we must pay much closer attention to what we have heard, so that we do not drift away from it, Hebrews 2:1.

For discussion

1. What important role do women play in society?

2. Read 4:1-5. Describe the actions of Israel's worship.

3. Read 4:4-5. What phrases give an indication of the motives of the people as they approached worship?

4. What five ways in 4:6-13 did God seek to move Israel back into compliance with the covenant?

5. In chapters four and five do you see any glimmer of hope for a chance of repentance from Israel? Why or why not?

6. What does wormwood stand for?

7. Had Israel given their heart to God, what would have characterized the nation? See 5:24.

8. Who did Sikkuth and Kiyyun represent?

9. Read 6:3-6. Describe the attitude of the people of Israel.

10. What would be God's response to the reveling and banqueting?

11. What stands out to you as an important lesson you can apply from Amos 4-6?

Amos 7-9: The Reasons for God's Judgment

Introduction

AFTER WARNING OF CERTAIN DESTRUCTION for grave disobedience on the part of the northern tribes, Amos begins to wrap up the book by speaking of five visions from the Lord God. Whether these were actual events that Amos saw or something God made known to him inwardly, we do not know.

The first vision, 7:1-3

In this vision Amos sees a locust-swarm forming. Was this a literal locust invasion such as in Joel's writing? Probably not. More likely, it is symbolic of what God would do because of Israel's continual rebellion. The late crop Amos refers to here is the crop that begins growing after the spring rains. (The growing season in the Middle East begins in October and continues through the winter months.) If the locusts took out the grass after the late crop came in, there was no hope for grass to grow substantially during the hot summer months. *The king's mowings* was probably referring to a tax levy placed on hay for the cavalry. As the locusts finish eating the grass, Amos prayed on behalf of the people seeking God's mercy, grace, and forgiveness. Israel was not as large, powerful, and influential as its people thought. They would not be able to recover easily from such a devastating locust plague. Verse three says that God relented and for a time took away the utter destruction He promised. Could the point of this vision be to show Israel that judgment would have come sooner had it not been for the prayers of the prophets and righteous people scattered throughout the land?

The second vision, 7:4-6

Later, God gave Amos a second vision in which he saw fire being poured out by God that devoured the land. This was not the usual kind of fire. This was the fire of judgment which lapped up the sea (the great deep) and was going to devour the land. Some have speculated that the phrase *devour the territory* refers to the newly acquired land in the north taken from Aram during the reign of Jeroboam II. This all-consuming fire was put out only because of the prayer of Amos who reminded God of their helplessness and dependence upon Him. Once again, God turns away from destruction. Could the first two visions be representative of the advances of the Assyrian army in the years leading up to Israel's final destruction in 722 B.C.? Tiglath-pileser led three campaigns between 734 and 732 B.C. that took away a good portion of Israel's territory. There is little doubt that the Assyrian general could have taken out the entire nation during these raids, but he held off for some reason. By 732 B.C., Israel had been reduced to little more than a vassal state with a puppet king who was required to pay heavy tribute to the Assyrian nation. 2 Kings 15:19-20 tells us that Menahem paid one thousand talents of silver as tribute to Pul (Tiglath-pileser). In commenting of this, Pul wrote the following in the historical records of the Assyrians:

> I received tribute from Menahem of Samaria…Like a bird, alone he fled and submitted to me.[1]

After a revolt in 722 B.C., Israel was completely absorbed into Assyria by Shalmaneser, 2 Kings 17:3-6.

The third vision, 7:7-9

In this vision God has a plumb line in His hand. A plumb line is a line with a weight on one end. This tool was used to assist builders judge the straightness of a wall vertically. Smith notes that "the plumb line was a symbol of judgment in the Old Testament," 2 Kings 21:13 and Isaiah 34:11.[2] In this vision Israel is the wall and the plumb line represents the law of God. At one time, Israel had been an upright nation, but now because of idolatry and rebellion the wall began to lean. Because of their spiritual instability, God determined that He could "no longer spare them." God said that time of pardon was passing away and they would be punished. The high places of Isaac refer to the altars erected to idols that dotted the landscape of Israel. They would be the first place to suffer the wrath of God. The idols that God's

The Dynasty of Jehu

KING	YEARS REIGNED
Jehu	841-814
Jehoahaz	814-798
Jehoash (Joash)	798-782
Jeroboam II	793-753
Zechariah	753

This is the word of the Lord which He spoke to Jehu, saying, "Your sons to the fourth generation shall sit on the throne of Israel." And so it was.
2 Kings 15:12

people toyed with all their existence would be unable to protect them against certain and swift destruction.

God also mentions the destruction of the house of Jeroboam II. Jeroboam II's great-grandfather, Jehu, was evil and followed in the idolatrous paths of his predecessors. 2 Kings 15:12 says that the sons of Jehu would rule over Israel for four generations. Jeroboam II was the third in line in this succession, and after his death, his son Zechariah reigned in his place. He was assassinated after just six months, 2 Kings 15:12. This brought an end to Jeroboam's ruling dynasty.

The reaction of the high priest

Amos' remarks concerning the royal family raised a response in the high priest of Israel, Amaziah. Amaziah quickly sends word to Jeroboam II. Amos was not seeking to overthrow the king; he was seeking to move the country into a religious awakening that would avert the judgment of God. Amaziah advises Amos to leave the country. It is interesting to note where Amos is prophesying when Amaziah confronts him. Verse thirteen tells us Amos was in Bethel, the very heart and worship center of the northern ten tribes. It could have been easy to rationalize that preaching in Bethel would have been ineffective at best. It was home to the national religion and important government officials dwelt there. We can infer from these verses that Amos was creating a following. How many "Bethels" are there in our day that we may have written off? There is power in the gospel message, and if we move in faith, God will bless us in our efforts.

Amaziah calls Amos a "seer" which is another name for prophets, and then tells him to go back to Judah and *there eat bread and there do your prophesying*. In commanding Amos to leave perhaps Amaziah was acting on direct authority of the king. The phrase *eat your bread* suggests that Amaziah thought Amos was prophesying for money. To that, Amos responds that he was not a professional prophet. The Lord took him from secular work and instructed him to go to Israel. The message of Amos came from the Lord. After Amaziah admonishes Amos not to prophesy, God said that his wife would become a harlot. When Israel fell into hard economic times, was she so wed to her material possessions and lifestyle that she would be willing to sell her body to keep everything she had acquired? Amos says the sons and daughters of Amaziah would die violently. Smith writes, "The fact that daughters would be included in the slaughter would indicate abnormal cruelty. Normally the Assyrians spared the women to become wives for their soldiers."[3] Finally, Amos says Amaziah would die in an "unclean" land. It would be taken over by the Assyrians. Israel would lose their land possession and be carried into exile. One can only wonder when these events began to play out in Amaziah's life if he recounted this exchange between himself and the prophet from Judah.

The fourth vision, 8:1-3

It is speculated that as we enter chapter eight Amos has returned to Judah. Here he continues his work in informing Israel of their fate. In the next vision Amos is shown a basket of summer fruit. Summer fruit would be symbolic of ripeness. The nation is ripe for judgment and destruction. *The end has come for My people Israel....* God would no longer spare them. An interesting contrast is to compare Amos 6:3-6 with Amos 8:3. Those who were at ease, reveling in wonderful material possessions and luxuries, would be subjected to wailing and terrible deaths.

Why Israel was ripe for destruction

Israel's sins were multiplied before the Lord. We read the following catalog of sins:

- 8:4 - Trampling the needy.
- 8:5 - Religious hypocrisy.
- 8:5 - Dishonest business dealings.
- 8:6 - Great oppression of the poor, so much that they had to pawn their clothing in order to purchase food not fit to eat.

To this God said He would not forget their sins. For this there would be certain punishment. The earth would quake as a sign of God's judgment. Is this the earthquake mentioned in Amos 1:1? There was a great earthquake during the reign of King Uzziah of Judah, and it was so severe that it was still being talked about two centuries later, Zechariah 14:5. The mention of the rising and fall of the Nile told Amos' listeners that this would be no minor event. The rising and fall of the Nile took weeks at a time. The tremors Amos mentions would go on for some time. In 8:9 Amos says that the sun [would] go down at noon and make the earth dark in broad daylight. On June 15, 763 B.C. there was a solar eclipse over the Middle East. Could this have been what Amos referred to? Maybe, but the more important message is symbolic. As drastic as it is to have darkness in the middle of the day, so it would be for Israel to fall from the pinnacle of economic and political prosperity to a conquered people as a scourge on the land.

A spiritual thirsting

As God would pour out His great destruction on His people and land, the people would begin to remember God and seek Him. Only this time He would not be there. He was going to remove His presence from them. The word pictures painted in these verses are graphic. Picture someone wandering aimlessly, desperate for God and the hope He delivers. They will not find hope because all hope is gone. They would finally realize their love for idols had created this problem. Dan (8:14) was in the northern reaches of Israel and had been a place of worship instituted by Jeroboam I, 1 Kings 12:29-30. Beersheba was one of the homes of Abraham. Evidently people had erected a shrine to idolatry in this city. There would be no hope in these idols. God had departed and they were left to reap the whirlwind.

The fifth vision

In the final vision in the book, Amos finds God standing beside the altar. What altar? Where? Jerusalem or Bethel? Most feel this altar was in Jerusalem because it is singular in nature. (There were many altars in Bethel to various deities.) No matter where the Lord is the message of this vision is that the destruction of the northern system of religion will take place. The *capitals* in 9:1 were ornaments on top of the pillars which held up the roof of the temple. The *threshold* refers to the doorsill. In other words, the temple would be shaken from top to bottom. There would be no escape. Those who were serving idols in the temple would be killed. Those who escaped the destruction in the temple would be hunted down like fugitives and executed. Even those who found themselves in captivity would be subject to execution. In 9:7, God says that Israel, the once great nation so beloved in the sight of God, was no different than the Ethiopians. The people could no longer rely upon their special status as the people of God. The time of protection and blessing from God had passed.

God would destroy the nation, but not the house of Jacob

While the nation would be taken away, a small remnant would remain to fulfill the promises made to Abraham. While the nation would be destroyed, not one righteous person would perish in the destruction, 9:9 *...But not a kernel will fall to the ground.* After the Day of the Lord, God would rebuild the house of David as it had been in the days of old. God would honor the promise He made to David in 2 Samuel 7:11-12, 16. There was a day coming when spiritual blessings through Jesus Christ would make people part of an everlasting kingdom, 8:14. There are some wonderful references to the church age in these verses. While all hope was lost for Israel's physical kingdom, God was moving forward with His plan to bring the Messiah and ultimately bless all the nations of the earth through Him.

Lessons for today

The power of the prayer of the righteous

In the first two visions certain destruction was held off because of the prayer of Amos. God listens to the prayers of the righteous. Consider all the good done and evil averted because of the prayer of the righteous. When we begin to realize the wonderful things that come about because of prayer, it will help us pray even more.

The power of the gospel in difficult places

How receptive would the people of Israel be to Amos' message? How out of place would a herdsman have been on the streets of Samaria? How would he have been regarded by the pious who worshipped in the temple at Bethel? Was Amos just wasting his time? By reading 7:10-17 it appears that Amos' teaching was creating quite a stir among the locals, perhaps even generating a following. How intimidated would we be to go into such a difficult place? The power we have is in God's word. Our job is to communicate the gospel and trust that it will fall on honest and sincere hearts.

Many will realize their great need for God only after it is too late

Amos 8:11-14 contains some of the saddest verses in all of Scripture. God was going to remove His presence from Israel. There would be no more opportunity to turn to Him. All hope had vanished. The people are left to roam around, desperately searching for the Lord, but He is not there. Unfortunately, their spiritual thirst would not be quenched. There is a coming time when God will once again turn away His presence. The souls that are cast into hell will have no hope of ever departing such a terrible place. It is a place of *weeping and gnashing of teeth,* Matthew 25:30. Some will realize only too late as to just how terrible hell will be.

For discussion

1. What took place in Amos' first vision? The second?

2. What caused God to relent on His punishment?

3. Explain the vision of the plumb line.

4. Who was Amaziah? What did he instruct Amos to do?

5. What was Amos' response to Amaziah?

6. What would come upon Amaziah and his family for telling Amos not to preach against Israel?

7. In Amos' fourth vision what was the summer fruit symbolic of?

8. List the sins found in 8:4-6. Would God overlook this?

9. What would be the sign of God's coming judgment? See 8:8-10.

10. What was Amos' fifth vision? What does it symbolize?

11. What are your thoughts and impressions on the book of Amos?

Chapter Endnotes

1 *Archaeology of Ancient Assyria.* www.bible-history.com. Website accessed December 11, 2006.

2 Smith, James E., *The Minor Prophets,* p. 188.

3 *Ibid.,* p. 192.

Lesson 10

Hosea 1-3: Hosea and Gomer

Introduction

IT IS GENERALLY THOUGHT that Hosea served as a priest in the Northern Kingdom. His name means "salvation" in the ancient Hebrew, and he has been long noted as a prophet who teaches us about the grace and mercy of God. It has been suggested that Hosea is a shortened form of a longer Hebrew name which means "God is Help." Hosea was a contemporary of Amos and lived during the prosperous eighth century B.C. Writing from his native land, Hosea's life is one of interest. Was his wife really a harlot? Why the odd names for his children? Was Hosea's marriage to Gomer ever reconciled? We know nothing of the early life of Hosea or what city he called home. From this book we do learn that he was a devoted servant of God who sought to impress upon the people the immense hurt and betrayal God felt at the conduct of the Israelites' addiction to idolatry.

Hosea's ministry began during the reign of Jeroboam II and most likely ended sometime before the northern tribes were destroyed by Assyria in 722 B.C. We know he was active in ministry before the end of the Jehu dynasty because he speaks of its punishment in Hosea 1:4. Hosea mentions four Judean kings as ruling during his time: Uzziah, Jotham, Ahaz, and Hezekiah all ruled during the latter part of the eighth century B.C. Why does Hosea mention only one king of Israel? An exact answer is unknown, but the kings that came after Jeroboam II in Israel experienced short-lived reigns and became increasingly weak. Hosea's silence on the annihilation of the north suggests that his ministry ended before 722 B.C.

Hosea had a distinct purpose in his ministry. Hosea 1:2 tells us that the prophet was directed to *take a wife of harlotry* and have children of harlotry. Was she "chaste" at the time of marriage? Most likely. Hailey points out that Gomer was most like a "woman of the age" who would have been brought up under the influence of idolatry and immorality. After the marriage ensued, she entered adulterous relationships allowing Hosea to personally relate to the hurt and betrayal God felt as His people committed spiritual adultery by worshipping idols. Hosea and Gomer had three children: Jezreel, Lo-ruhamah, and Lo-ammi. What must his family life have been like?

The times of Hosea

While the ministries of Hosea and Amos overlap somewhat, it appears that much of Hosea's ministry came in the period after Amos was directed to go back to Judah by Amaziah, Amos 7:10-17. Much of the book is said to reflect the times after Tiglath-pileser took away much of the Northern Kingdom (2 Kings 15:29) leaving Ephraim as the primary tribe of those that remained. Religiously, things continued to deteriorate. While they may have worshipped the Lord in pretense, their main concern was with idolatry. Knowledge of God had been lost; corruption and ignorance of the laws of God were prevalent. Worship to Baal had fully permeated the society and contributed to gross immorality. The people had completely rejected God. Socially and morally the nation found itself in a cesspool. Chapters four, six, and thirteen describe some of the conditions of the day. In a land of people who were told to be separate, distinct, and set apart from the other nations around them, Israel now had completely fallen away from God.

The World of Hosea

TIME	ISRAEL			JUDAH	
	KING		PROPHET	KING	PROPHET
760			JONAH (780-760)		
750	JEROBOAM II (793-753)	* Zechariah ruled for 8 months in 753. Assassinated by Shallum who ruled for 1 month in 752. Shalom assassinated by Menahem.	AMOS (760-750)	UZZIAH (792-740)	
740	MENAHEM (752-742)			JOTHAM (750-732)	* Jotham was co-regent with Uzziah for 10 years. ISAIAH (762-690)
730	PEKAH (742-732)	* Pekahiah ruled from 742-740.	HOSEA (750-725)		
720	HOSHEA (732-722)			AHAZ (JEHOSOPHAT) (735-716)	MICAH (735-700)
710	Northern Kingdom Destroyed by Assyria				
700	722 BC			HEZEKIAH (716-687)	

These were also times of great political upheaval. After the long, stable, and prosperous reign of Jeroboam II, things quickly changed. Jeroboam II's son, Zechariah took over the throne, but reigned only six months before being assassinated by Shallum, 2 Kings 15:8-12. Shallum could only maintain power for one month before being taken out by Menahem, 2 Kings 15:13. Menahem was most likely in charge of the troops in Tirzah, one of the king's residences. Hearing of Zechariah's murder, he traveled to Samaria and killed

Shallum. Menahem quickly sought to establish his power and dominance over the nation by striking the cities that refused loyalty to him. He attacked Tiphsah, *ripping up all its women who were with child*, 2 Kings 15:16. He ruled ten years in Samaria. While Menahem is ruling, Tiglath-pileser (Pul) from Assyria begins to assert his dominance. (Tiglath-pileser was the name Pul took when he became the king of Assyria.) Assyria exacted a heavy tariff on the people to keep from being destroyed. This must have had a crippling effect on the rich of society as the good times they enjoyed in the previous decades had quickly come to an end, 2 Kings 15:19-20.

After the reign of Menahem, his son Pekahiah ruled in his place for two years. That is about all we are told concerning his reign. He was murdered by Pekah who succeeded him to the throne. In writing about Pekahiah, Josephus notes: He followed the barbarity of his father, and so ruled but two years only, after which he was slain by his friends at a feast, by the treachery of one Pekah, the general of his horse, and the son of Remaliah who laid snares for him.[1]

During Pekah's reign, 2 Kings 15:29 says that Tiglath-pileser began carrying off the northern parts of the kingdom as captives. Ephraim, Issachar, and half of Manasseh were all that were left in the Northern Kingdom. To fight back the Assyrians, Pekah and Rezin (the ruler of Syria), formed an alliance. They implored Ahaz, king of Judah, to join them to which he refused, Isaiah 7. After his refusal, Israel and Syria declared war on Judah. They inflicted heavy casualties on Judah. Israel even carried the Judeans into slavery, 2 Chronicles 28:8. Things were so bad for Ahaz that he allied himself with Assyria, who responded by attacking Syria and killing Rezin, 2 Kings 16:9.

2 Kings 15:30 says that Hoshea conspired against Pekah, killed him, and ruled in his place. This conspiracy was at the hands of Assyria. In official Assyrian writing Tiglath-pileser said, "Pekah I slew, Hoshea I appointed over them."[2] Hoshea would be the last king of the Northern Kingdom. He would "reign" for nine years. Six years into his reign, he was found guilty of conspiring against the Assyrians and placed into prison. Beginning in 725 B.C., Assyria began what would become a three-year siege of Samaria. Hoshea is not mentioned again. The Northern Kingdom finally fell in December, 722 B.C.

The above paragraphs demonstrate the times of Hosea. Picture a nation in chaos, dark clouds of uncertainty rising with the onslaught of Assyrian aggression, murder and conspiracy, and no thought given to God or His power. It is an extremely sad ending to what had been a glorious nation just a few centuries before.

Hosea presents a contrast with Amos

Throughout Hosea a consistent theme is portrayed showing God's love for those who turn their back on Him. Hosea is known as a preacher of mercy who stresses God's special relationship with Israel. Through his own personal hurt, caused by the infidelity of Gomer, Hosea relates the hurt God experienced because of the treachery of idolatry and trusting in human alliances. Despite the unfaithfulness of God's people, God still loved them and desired to see them do right. This stands in stark contrast to Amos who prophesied to the Northern Kingdom in the 750's B.C. Amos stressed God's wrath was going to be poured out because of violence, idolatry, and immorality. Amos seems to indicate that God had reached a point where the mercy and longsuffering of God would reach an end, removing His presence from them, Amos 8:11-14. There was a place for both men. Both served the purposes of God. These two books give us a glimpse of the nature of God— His goodness and severity, His love and His justice.

Hosea's family life

In Hosea 1:2, God commands Hosea to take a *wife of harlotry and have children of harlotry; for the land commits flagrant harlotry, forsaking the LORD.* What is a *wife of harlotry*? Most likely, she was not a harlot when Hosea married her, but became one later. This makes sense if one keeps in mind the parallel between Hosea and Gomer and the Lord and Israel. Israel did not start out in harlotry, but soon moved to it after entering a covenant with God. His wife would have been someone who grew up in the Israelite culture of the day—influenced by idolatry and loose morals. Abandoning the covenant she made with her husband would not have been that serious in her eyes.

Gomer's Children

CHILD	HEBREW MEANING
Jezreel	*God will scatter or God will sow*
Lo-ruhamah	*no mercy*
Lo-ammi	*not my people*

Hosea went out as God directed and found a wife. Gomer was the daughter of Diblaim. After their marriage, Hosea and Gomer have a child: Jezreel. "Jezreel" means *God scatters*. The name can also mean God sows. Smith notes that "in Hebrew the name Jezreel sounds very much like the name Israel." "Israel" which means "Prince of God" would become "Jezreel," scattered by God. [3] The house of Jehu mentioned in 1:4 is the dynasty of four kings that was mentioned in 2 Kings 10:30-31; 15:12. It would be destroyed because of the bloodshed of Jezreel. This is a reference back to Jehu's destruction on the house of Ahab, something God had sanctioned in 2 Kings 9:1-10. While Jehu moved according to God's will to destroy the ruling family of Ahab, it was not with God-glorifying motives. Jehu's conquest was particularly bloody. See 2 Kings 9:21-28, 30-37; 10:1-10. Not only would the house of Jehu be broken, but the entire nation would come to an end. Their armies would be defeated in the Valley of Jezreel. This was a valley where many famous battles took place.

Contrasts and Important Lessons of Hosea 1-3

The Symbolism of Gomer's Children

	JEZREEL	LO-RUHAMAH	LO-AMMI
Hebrew Meaning	*God will scatter*	*no mercy*	*not my people*
Immediate Application	Israel would be destroyed & scattered, 1:4	Israel would have no mercy as it was being destroyed, 1:6	God's relationship with Israel was over, 1:9
A Time Was Coming When	God would sow & His people would be gathered together, 1.11	God's people would be shown mercy, 2:19	the people would become God's possession, 2:23

Gomer conceived again and gave birth to a daughter: Lo-ruhamah, 1:6-7. The name "Lo-ruhamah" means "no mercy." God would no longer have mercy on His people. God would no longer overlook their extreme rebelliousness and disregard for the law of God. There has been some question on whether Lo-ruhamah could call Hosea her father. Is this child by another man? We are not told for sure. Hosea 1:7 tells us of God's compassion on Judah, at least at this point. They would not be destroyed by the Assyrian aggression. The only way Judah was not destroyed was through the power of God, not through its own military or political capability.

After Lo-ruhamah was weaned, Gomer conceived again and gave birth to a son. God commanded Hosea to name the son Lo-ammi which means "not My people." God had cut Himself off from the people. Israel had violated the covenant relationship for so long that finally God had endured enough. The relationship He had with them was over.

After a period of punishment and exile, there would come a time when God would reestablish a remnant. This is what is under discussion in Hosea 1:10-2:1. It is important to note that verse one of chapter two is best understood in the context at the end of chapter one. In these verses God reasserts that even though the nation of Israel was about to be destroyed, the promises to Abraham, Isaac, and Jacob would still be carried out. This has come to pass with the establishment of the church and the preaching of the gospel to all nations. Peter and Paul spoke extensively of the blessings that came to both

Jew and Gentile through Jesus Christ. This was a direct fulfillment of God's promise to Abraham in Genesis 12:3. Israel and Judah and all men would be brought together as one—through Jesus Christ. These are those who would receive and be benefactors of the mercy of God, 2:1. "Ruhamah" speaks of those who have obtained mercy. This mercy is possible because of the blood shed by Jesus.

Spiritual adultery

A prominent theme in Hosea is that idolatry is the same as spiritual adultery. In 2:2-7 God turns His attention to the nation of Israel. What Hosea dealt with in experiencing the betrayal of Gomer, so God was dealing with the same betrayal by Israel. In this metaphor God is pictured as the husband and Israel the unfaithful bride. God is ending His relationship with Israel because of their unfaithfulness. Because of Israel's treachery, there was no basis to continue the relationship. God warns that if the nation did not put *away* (its) *harlotry* that He would *strip her naked*. Smith writes, "Some evidence suggests that women who broke marriage vows were first stripped naked before they were executed."[4] She (Israel) would find herself back in the same condition before God found her, took her in, and cared for her. All the physical blessings they took for granted would be removed. God was going to make it impossible for them to restore their physical blessings once they lost them. The phrase *she will pursue her lovers* is particularly interesting. As Assyria moved in on the nation, Israel would pursue worship to idols even more calling upon them for deliverance. Unable to find satisfaction and realizing their desperate situation they would seek to return to God, *for it was better for me then than now,* 2:7. Only this time God would not be there for He would remove His presence from them, Amos 8:10-14.

Israel forgot the source of her blessings

God is the one who bestowed the rich physical blessings on Israel. The grain, fresh wine, oil, silver, and gold all came from God. Perhaps the ultimate insult was that Israel took these very same blessings and used them in the advancement of idolatry. God says that He is going to take away these blessings, Hosea 2:9. Their great dependence upon the Lord was going to be realized—only this time it would be too late. Even if Israel sought assistance from its allies, there would be no help: *no one will rescue her out of My hand,* 2:10.

All the festivities that Hosea witnessed as he prophesied would come to a crushing end. God would put an end *to all her gaiety, her feasts, her new moons, her Sabbaths, and all her festal assemblies,* 2:11. The devastation would be so complete that there would be nothing for anyone to celebrate. No happiness would be in the land. Everything that the people trusted in—their idols, prosperity, social and political status—would be taken away. It is important to stress that these things were not for some far-off generation long after Hosea—what he prophesied about took place within a few decades. How hard it must have been for the people to imagine that the fertile land which grew their crops would *become a forest and the beasts of the field will [would] devour them,* 2:12. As Hosea preached, how many cast him off as preaching the unthinkable?

A reason to hope

At the conclusion of chapter one God alludes to a future time when a remnant would be blessed by God. As Hosea brings chapter two to a close, he speaks of a future time when God would seek to win His people back to Him. In these verses we get a glimpse of God's great love and mercy. Time and time again God had an opportunity to give up on mankind, but He continues to return, offering an opportunity to be reconciled, hoping for the best. Hosea 2:14-23 looks ahead to a future time when the remnant would be led out of captivity and return to their homeland. Ultimately, there are some applications in these verses that would be fulfilled during the "church age."

Hosea likens the upcoming punishment and destruction to a journey of going back to Egypt, which represented slavery and bondage. Metaphorically, God would once again lead His people out of Egypt into the wilderness giving His people a new chance to experience His blessings and grace. God longed for a true relationship with them as symbolized by calling Him Ishi or "my husband." No longer would her allegiance be to Baal, as symbolized in 2:16. In this time Israel would totally cut off her desire to worship Baal.

Hosea 2:18 looks ahead to the covenant God made with His people through Jesus Christ. Much in 2:18 parallels Isaiah's writing in Isaiah 11:1-11. The peace here is that which comes through Christ. As we mentioned in lesson three, Old Testament terms are being used to describe New Testament concepts. During the church age, God's people are crowned in righteousness, justice, lovingkindness, and compassion. It will be a time marked by spiritual Israel's faithfulness to God.

In these verses we note the desire of God to have a relationship with His creation: mankind. In 2:8 *know* is used in the New American Standard Version for the first of many times in this book. Israel lacked an intimate relationship with God, and this caused them to be ignorant of the fact that God had showered them with many blessings. In speaking of a future time (specifically 2:20-23) a close, personal, and intimate relationship is foreseen. This is what God has desired all along. God would hear the prayers of His people and shower them with wonderful spiritual blessings. God would show *compassion on her who had not obtained compassion, And I will say to those who were not My people, 'You are My people! And they will say, 'You are my God!* In *that time,* God would have fellowship with both Jew and Gentile. And that relationship would be one that is touching, special, and intimate.

Hosea takes Gomer back

After looking ahead to a future time, we move back to eighth century Israel in the beginning part of chapter three. Hosea is commanded by God to go back to a woman *who is loved by her husband, yet an adulteress.* Many think the "woman" in 3:1 is Gomer. Perhaps Gomer had been cast out of the home by Hosea for her unfaithfulness. Could she have become a temple prostitute? Whatever the case, at the end of verse one the comparison is made to God who continued to love His people despite their ungodliness and rebellion. Raisin cakes (3:1) were most likely used in idol worship.

After moving out of Hosea's house, Gomer must have worn out her attractiveness as a prostitute and found herself mired in slavery. Hosea bought her back for *fifteen shekels of silver and a homer and a half of barley,* 3:2. Upon bringing her home Hosea laid down specific expectations. Gomer was not to have sexual relations with anyone – including Hosea. A period of discipline is in view here. It was to be temporary in nature with an end view of full restoration of all the rights and privileges of the relationship in the future. *Stay* (NASB) or *abide* (ASV) are used in other places to describe the period of waiting for purification after childbirth, Leviticus 12:4-5.[5]

Likewise, Israel would have to suffer through a discipline period without a king or the ability to practice religion of any kind—true worship or idol worship. Because of this period of discipline, Hosea looks forward to a time when Israel would *return and seek the LORD…and come trembling to the Lord and to His goodness in the last days,* 3:5. This period of discipline would finally break them of the idolatry that had plagued their existence since the beginning.

The message of the first three chapters of this book cannot be underemphasized. The physical relationship and problems between Hosea and Gomer symbolized the spiritual relationship and problems between God and Israel. Israel had committed spiritual adultery and would be destroyed. For a period, they would experience discipline and chastening. But there would come a time when they would be restored to experience many spiritual blessings in *the last days.*

For discussion

1. Hosea's name means what? He was from:

2. When did Hosea's ministry begin?

3. Describe the religious and social conditions of Hosea's day.

4. Describe the political condition of Hosea's day.

5. Are there any constant themes running through the book of Hosea?

6. Hosea and Amos were contemporaries. Show how the two books are similar   Show how the two books are different.

7. Who was Hosea's wife and what character trait is she most known for?

8. Name the three children Gomer gave birth to. What do their names mean?

9. Do you believe Hosea was the father of all three children? Why or why not?

10. Who gave Israel all she had? Did Israel remember this?

11. After a period of discipline, what would happen to Israel?

12. Describe the blessings to come in the last days as detailed by Hosea.

13. What are some spiritual lessons we can learn from Hosea 1-3?

Chapter Endnotes

1   Flavius Josephus, *Antiquities of the Jews*, p. 294

2   *International Standard Bible Encyclopedia*, Electronic Database Copyright (c)1996 by Biblesoft)

3   Smith, James E., The Minor Prophets, p. 211

4   Smith, James E., The Minor Prophets, p. 214

5   Hubbard, David Allan, Hosea, p. 93

Hosea 4-8:
God's Dispute with Israel

Introduction

BEGINNING IN CHAPTER FOUR Hosea begins a new section of the book. While Hosea is hard to organize into a clear, concise outline, this section resembles a court scene where God calls His people to court because of their violation of the covenant agreement they made with Him when they entered the Promised Land. God had a controversy with them because there was a lack of faithfulness, kindness, and knowledge of God in the land. As we go through the remainder of Hosea's book, he deals with each one of these points in reverse order beginning with Israel's lack of knowledge of God.

Israel's Great Sins

HOSEA 4:2
swearing
deception
murder
stealing
adultery
violence
revenge (bloodshed follows bloodshed)

This lack of knowledge led to some specific sins committed by the people. These are listed in 4:2-5. Check out the sins listed in the table. God says that nature testifies of the sins of the people. This could be in reference to the witnesses called upon when Israel entered the covenant with God many generations before. Deuteronomy 30:19 says, *I call heaven and earth to witness against you today, that I have set before you life and death, the blessing and the curse.* Every part of nature was suffering because of the sins of the nation. The disappearing fish in the sea would indicate that severe drought gripped the land. The people were so hardened in their sin that there was no pleading with them. That time had passed. When the nation would be destroyed, there would be no escape—day or night.

Responsibility for the condition of the people not only rested with themselves, but it also fell squarely upon the priests. God singles them out for condemnation in 4:6-10. They failed to instruct and train the people in the ways of the Lord. Because they rejected knowledge, they would be rejected from being priests and their children would be forgotten by the Lord. The priesthood had become very prosperous and influential during the reign of Jeroboam II. They were corrupt and served God superficially. They even delighted in the sins of the people as that would give them more of the best of the meat from sacrifices to feast upon. The priests, like the people, were not going to be exempt from certain punishment. They would be repaid for their deeds, 4:9-10.

More sins

Beginning in 4:11 we note some extreme sins committed by the people which were repugnant in the sight of God. *Harlotry* had become commonplace among the people due to general immorality and the worship of Baal. Drunkenness was condemned because it *takes away the understanding*. Hailey writes that *wine and new wine* had to do with fermented grape juice. "New wine indicates fermented wine with the ability to intoxicate."[1] In this state of decreased or non-existent understanding, the people turned to idols constructed of wood and superstitious black magic. The *diviner's wand* was probably a practice where two rods were held up vertically and then allowed to drop as the medium uttered a chant. "The oracle was inferred from the way the sticks fell whether forward, backward, to the right, or to the left."[2] Idolatry was practiced on the top of every hill. Canaanite people felt higher elevations would bring them closer to their deities. Because of their participation in these idolatrous acts, the people of Israel were said to have committed spiritual adultery, 4:13. Not only were the people guilty of spiritual adultery in violating their covenant with God, they were also guilty of physical adultery. Men thought nothing of joining themselves to temple prostitutes, and their daughters gladly participated in the temple rites that glorified sexual gratification, 4:14.

Judah beware!

As Hosea prophesies primarily to Israel, he does not fail to leave out Judah. Judah also had to deal with idolatry throughout its existence, and within one hundred forty years of Hosea it too would be destroyed and carried off into captivity. The worship of idols was one of the principal reasons. In 4:15-16, Judah is warned not to go off into idolatry and not be like their brother Israel who is called a stubborn heifer. This reference is to the closed heart of the people and their obstinance in refusing to go along with God's expectations in living up to the covenant which they agreed to. The reference to a lamb in a large field (4:16) tells Israel that God's veil of protection was being removed. Just as a lamb would be extremely vulnerable to an attack by a predator while grazing in a large field, so Israel would be left exposed to be overtaken by its enemies.

Judah was told to leave Israel alone. Ephraim (the most influential province in Israel at the time of Hosea's writing) had joined himself to idols. The language in verse seventeen involves an intimate relationship like that of the marriage relationship. Ephraim had forsaken her true husband, the Lord, and joined herself to Baal and other Canaanite gods. Ultimately, they would be brought down because of their sin. God could no longer tolerate their violation of the covenant.

Pride goes before destruction

In 5:1, Hosea calls the attention of the people once again. They needed to give heed to what he was about to say because the judgment of God applied to them. The people were caught in their own sin and all that awaited them was destruction. Everyone in the kingdom was going to be subject to this judgment: common people, the king, the priests—everyone! Mizpah was located east of the Jordan in Gilead and Mt. Tabor was in the west near Nazareth. People on both sides of the Jordan would be subject to this judgment because of deep depravity. All would be chastised, 5:2.

Israel would not be able to escape the punishment as they were not hidden from God. Their hearts were completely aligned against repentance—the sweet taste of sin had dulled their senses for truth. Pride blinded Israel from seeing their dependence upon God. They looked at their country, power, might, money, and physical surroundings and took all the credit. Pride goes before destruction, Proverbs 16:18! Israel would stumble in their iniquity, 5:5. The Southern Kingdom would also fall for its pride and stubbornness, but God would allow them more time because they were not as hardened in sin as their brothers to the north.

God would remove His presence from them

Some of the saddest words in the Old Testament are found in 5:6-15. After God began to bring judgment on His people, the people would be awakened from their spiritual sleep and search for God. They would not find Him. *He has withdrawn from them*, 5:6. Looking back over their history, Israel had a very repetitive cycle where they fell out of favor with God because of unfaithfulness (idolatry). God would send in a nation to oppress and afflict them. After suffering at the hands of the aggressors, the nation would suddenly "get religion" and cry out to God for relief. He would raise a deliverer to carry them out of the oppression and for the remainder of that generation the nation would serve the Lord. Once that generation died off the cycle would repeat itself. If Israel hoped that they would be able to call out to God for deliverance from Assyrian aggression, there was no hope this time. God would allow them to be destroyed as punishment for their sin.

Know or *Knowledge* in Hosea

REFERENCE	COMMENTS
Hosea 2:8	*Israel did not know it was God who blessed them*
Hosea 2:20	*God desired a close and personal relationship*
Hosea 4:1	*no knowledge of God in the land*
Hosea 4:6	*people would be destroyed for a lack of knowledge*
Hosea 5:3	*God knew their ways*
Hosea 5:4	*Israel guilty of spiritual harlotry & did not know the Lord*
Hosea 6:3	*Israel claimed to know God but only knew Him superficially*
Hosea 6:6	*God delights in knowledge*
Hosea 8:2	*Israel would cry out in distress, but no one to save them*
Hosea 13:4	*Israel was not to "know" any other gods*
Hosea 14:9	*we need to know the way of God*

In these verses Ephraim is the focus. It should be viewed as being representative for the nation of Israel as a whole. For much of Hosea's later ministry Ephraim would be the largest tribe left since Assyria had annexed most of the nation. As Assyria marched in, Israel would be tempted to better its position by making agreements with the invaders. It is thought that 5:13 is a reference to Menahem's agreement to pay high tariffs to Pul to keep the nation from being destroyed. Refer to 2 Kings 15:19. *King Jareb* was another name for the King of Assyria. King Jareb literally means "king striver" or "king contention." The king of Assyria was not going to help Israel out, making deals with him only increased Israel's problems exponentially. God was going to be to both nations as *a lion.* There *would be none to deliver.* Again, any false hope of God changing His mind at the last moment was too far gone. God would remove Himself to *His place* until the period of exile humbled them, and they would earnestly seek Him, 5:15.

Many people are confused by the wording of the first few verses of Hosea 6. Should 6:1-3 be placed at the end of chapter five? Should these verses be viewed as genuine repentance by the people? Or is this a sarcastic response by the people where they feel that if the Assyrian aggressors overtake them, God will surely come to their rescue if they "repent." This author tends to lean toward these verses indicating "superficial" repentance. They most likely felt that when they began to be squeezed by the Assyrian expansion, all they had to do was call out to God and He would shorten the time of their punishment. This position is backed up by the wording in 6:4: *What shall I do with you, O Ephraim? What shall I do with you, O Judah? For your loyalty is like a morning cloud and like the dew which goes away early,* 6:4. In verse four we get a glimpse of the extreme hurt and betrayal experienced by God at Israel's rejection of Him. This was personal with God. Because of their fleeting obedience, God sent prophets who warned of destruction and judgment.

God's true desire

Hosea 6:6 is a very powerful verse. *For I delight in loyalty rather than sacrifice, and in the knowledge of God rather than burnt offerings.* God wants a real relationship with His people. He wants our genuine love. It is the kind of love that manifests itself in righteousness, 1 John 3:18. It is an *agape* type of love that is commanded in the New Testament, John 13:34-35. This is what God has always wanted from His creation. Sacrifices (under the Old Testament law) and religious acts of service (under the New Testament law) mean nothing without a connection of love and adoration for the Creator. If that is missing, God will reject the sacrifices and worship every time.

As you read 6:7-11, remember that this is "personal" with God. The betrayal and hurt are real. Read these verses from this perspective. They rejected righteousness and embraced sin. Entire cities had been given over to wickedness. Even priests were guilty of murder! Shechem was a city of refuge located between Bethel and Samaria. Bethel was the religious center of the Northern Kingdom while Samaria was the capitol. Those who would be traveling to Bethel would be carrying items to be offered for sacrifice which would have been easy prey for priests or anyone who wished to rob people of their belongings.

A corrupt political situation

Chapter seven gives us Hosea's perspective on the political upheaval that characterized his times. Assyria was increasing its influence over the region and there was betrayal, mayhem, and murder in Israel's political establishment. It is suspected that 7:3-7 gives us insight on the background behind Pekah's assassination of Pekahiah in 740 B.C. In these verses the friends and acquaintances of the king betray him, secretly plotting his murder and the overthrow of his government. Pekahiah's father, Menahem, had agreed to pay heavy tariffs to the Assyrians in exchange for remaining in power and having some independence. The wealthiest families in the kingdom were required to pay this tariff, 2 Kings 15:19-20. The payments to Assyria continued in Pekahiah's reign and the wealthy class revolted. During much of Pekahiah's reign Assyria was preoccupied with other matters and did not flex their military muscles as much. Pekah and his associates were motivated by anti-Assyrian sentiment and plotted against the king. Pekahiah was assassinated in 740 B.C.

After Pekah began his rule, he immediately began to move the nation into an anti-Assyrian stance. Pekah began reaching out to his neighbors in efforts to form an alliance against Assyria. Aram (Syria) and Egypt were the primary partners in this alliance (see 7:11). Pekah and Rezin (the leader of Syria) implored Judah to join this alliance, and when Ahaz (King of Judah) refused, Pekah and Rezin go to war with Judah. Hosea's wording in 7:8 explains the situation: *Ephraim mixes himself with the nations...strangers devour his strength, yet he does not know it*. While Israel desperately reaches out to its neighbors, no thought whatsoever is given to God. They had been called to be separate from the other nations and depend upon God. As they turned to other nations, their uniqueness as a nation was completely lost. While they felt they were increasing their strength by forming alliances, their strength was being depleted. God was going to bring His judgment against them, *I will bring them down like the birds of the sky*, 7:12. Woe was coming to them because they forgot God. *Destruction is theirs, for they have rebelled against Me*, 7:13.

In 7:14-16 we see another example of God's broken heart. God wanted true repentance. Instead of crying out for Him, they were concerned only with their physical blessings being taken away. God had trained and strengthened them. He gave them great power over their enemies. Yet they turned their advantages into opportunities to sin. As Assyria clamped down on them with pressure, they looked to everyone but God. *They turn, but not upward*, 7:16. Because of this, they would perish. The alliance they built with Egypt would not sustain them against the overwhelming power of Assyria. In 734 B.C. Tiglath-pileser invaded Gaza and had victory against the Egyptian forces there. If Israel was counting on Egypt for strategic protection, all hope faded when Assyria subdued the forces of the African nation.

Israel will reap the whirlwind

In Hosea's day the trumpet was used to call men to war. Assyria, like an eagle, was going to come down upon them with no warning. This was because of their rebellion against the law of God. They violated the covenant they made with Him so many generations before. As the destruction ensued, they would call out to God, we know you…but for all intents…they did not. Their lack of respect and reverence for Him had driven God away…for good. When Hosea says Israel has rejected the good, Hosea was saying that as a nation Israel detested good. Because of this, *the enemy* [would] *pursue him,* 8:3.

For generations Israel had gone about things their way, seeking no assistance from God. They placed kings in power without seeking spiritual counsel. They set up an unauthorized religious system and initiated religious practices associated with it. They claimed this was all to worship the Lord. Here God disassociates Himself with their worship. *With their silver and gold they have made idols for themselves…. He has rejected your calf, O Samaria,* 8:4-5. But this time God was incensed with their lack of purity: *how long will they be incapable of innocence?* It had been quite some time since they had lived righteously before the Lord. Because of their sowing to the wind, they would reap the whirlwind. They would get more than they bargained for. This is the deal that is always made with sin. Sin always brings out more consequences than bargained for. What had yet to be swallowed up by Assyria would be very soon. Their days were numbered.

God condemns their alliances with foreign nations. Israel aligned itself with Assyria in its waning years to keep from being cut off completely. God would no longer accept their sacrificial gifts and would remember only their iniquity. Hosea 8:14 is especially important in understanding God's hurt. *For Israel has forgotten his Maker.* If one gets to the bottom of the matter, the root of Israel's sin comes to their having forgotten God. They turned their backs on Him. This time they were too far gone to save. The end was coming.

For discussion

1. What are some of the specific sins committed by the people listed in 4:2-5?

2. Describe the status and position of the priests during Hosea's day.

3. Why is knowledge of God vitally important?

4. What was a diviner's wand?

5. How prevalent was idolatry at this time? Did they feel ashamed for openly worshipping idols? What does this say about the progression of sin?

6. Why was Israel called a stubborn heifer?

7. How was Israel a lamb in a large field?

8. What blinded Israel from seeing their dependence upon God?

9. Who was King Jareb?

10. Do you think the repentance in 6:1-3 is genuine? Why or why not?

11. What in Hosea 4-8 makes the reader see God's personal and deep hurt over Israel's treachery?

12. What did God really desire from His people?

13. What would happen to Israel because of their trust in other nations?

14. How can Israel's reaping the whirlwind help us live better spiritual lives?

Chapter Endnotes

1   Hailey, Homer E., *A Commentary on the Minor Prophets* (Louisville, KY: Religious Supply, 1993), p. 150.

2   Smith, James E., *The Minor Prophets*, p. 231.

Hosea 9-11: Israel Will Meet with Destruction

Introduction

AS WE MOVE INTO CHAPTER NINE of Hosea, God's message to the people is that they will experience great tribulation and distress at the hands of Assyria. Because of their great sin, they would be thrown out of the land of promise and made captives in enemy territory. This would end all reasons for rejoicing. Some believe that 9:1 gives us insight to the relief the people felt after the withdrawal of the Assyrians for a few years during the reign of Menahem. 2 Kings 15:20 says that Tiglath-pileser withdrew his troops after Menahem agreed to pay tribute to Assyria. While there is little doubt that the people did not like paying tribute, that was much better than having enemy troops moving to and fro throughout the land. Is this the rejoicing that Hosea mentions in 9:1?

Assyrian Kings During the 8th Century B.C.

KING	REIGN	COMMENTS	PROPHETS
Adad-Nirari III	806-783	Assyrian rule weakens	Joel
Shalmaneser IV	782-773		Jonah?
Ashur-Dan III	772-755	Internal conflict / rebellion in the kingdom	Jonah?
Ashur-Nirari V	754-745		Amos, Isaiah
Tiglath-pileser III	745-727	Regains Assyrian might	Hosea
Shalmaneser V	726-722	Captures Samaria; deports Israelites	Hosea? Micah?
Sargon II	721-705	Captures Egypt, Urartu, died in battle	Isaiah
Sennacherib	704-681	Overtook Babylon	the people would become God's possession, 2:23

In their worship to idols Israel had begun to believe that the gods were blessing their nation with good harvests and material blessings. The more material blessings they received the more they worshipped the Baals. Hosea says that God would take away the material blessings they coveted. *Threshing floor and wine press will not feed them, And the new wine will fail them,* 9:2. Because of their gross spiritual adultery, the people would *not remain in the LORD'S land.* They were about to lose the possession God gave them. In 9:3, when God mentions that *Ephraim will return to Egypt,* He does not mean that they would literally return to Egypt. The people would become as they were in Egypt: slaves held in captivity against their will. Previously in this study, we have noted the extreme brutality of the Assyrians. Life as a slave in their country was no picnic. They often boasted of the cruel treatment they dished out on their captives. While in captivity, Israel would be forced to *eat unclean food.* They would lose all privilege to worship freely. They would be unable to offer sacrifices that were acceptable to God and worshiping Him would only stir of memories of what had been. Gone would be their feast days and the great joy that was often associated with them. These things were part of the high cost of idolatry and the sin associated with it.

In verses six and seven we see that Israel would suffer a complete loss of hope. All the things they held dear would be taken over by their enemy. All the wonderful homes, palaces, and cities would be grown up. Hosea says, *the days of punishment have come, The days of retribution have come...* He speaks of them as already happening. Indeed, they were. By this time Assyria had already been on the march subduing over half their country. Their king had been reduced to puppet status and all the prestige that had been associated with the kingdom had disappeared. Only too late would they realize that the false prophets who had been "prophesying" smooth words were fools. In its waning days Israel had only wanted to hear that which was pleasant. Turning deaf ears to the genuine prophets of the Lord they rushed headlong into destruction. God was going to remember their iniquity and *punish their sins,* 9:9.

Great was their fall

God mentions how He first found Israel: *Like grapes in the wilderness.* They were something that had been greatly desired, but they soon devoted themselves to Baal. The reference to *Baal-peor* is a reference to the events in Numbers 25 when the Israelites joined themselves to the religion of Moab. What we worship does influence us. As Israel gave themselves over to lust and wantonness, it was reflected in every aspect of their life. *And they became as detestable as that which they loved,* 9:10.

Along with their destruction, Israel would find its population greatly diminished. Ancient Jewish culture valued childbirth and looked upon it as a blessing from God, Psalm 127:3-4. Now there would be no birth, *no pregnancy, and no conception,* 9:11. If a child was managed to be brought up, it would be fatherless. This great woe was coming because God withdrew His presence from them. This stands in direct contrast with what God wished for His people. He had wanted them to be a wonderful, secure, prosperous, and godly nation. But instead of being raised for honor, *Ephraim will bring out his children for slaughter,* 9:13. The Assyrians would march in and kill those they did not take into captivity. Verse fourteen is most likely an interjection by Hosea himself where he asks God to pour out His judgment against the people. They deserved the punishment they were going to receive. In verse fifteen Hosea mentions Gilgal. Gilgal occupies a very notable place in Jewish history. It was a place where God bestowed numerous blessings on the people as testimony to His mercy and grace. But now acts of evil were committed in this place. See Hosea 4:15; 12:1 and Amos 4:4; 5:5. Because of this, God would *drive them out of My [His] house,* 9:15. What was prophesied in verses sixteen and seventeen came to pass. The inhabitants of the Northern Kingdom were absorbed into the Assyrian nation and were scattered throughout the Middle East. Their national identity was stricken and the nation they remembered was cast into history forever.

Israel's gods would be unable to deliver them

God had richly blessed Israel. The bounty of their harvests was not arguable. But as their harvests increased, so did their sin against God. Instead of recognizing where the blessings came from, they gave the glory to the idols they served. While they may have claimed to serve the Lord, their actions proved otherwise. God was going to *break down their altars and destroy their sacred pillars,* 10:2. As calamity began to spread, is 10:3 a forecast of their recognition that they would realize the folly in their actions? The kings they installed without God's authority were powerless to stop the aggression. Some would only realize too late that they had put themselves in this position because of their spiritual adultery. Their kings were worthless, speaking vain words. Could this be in reference to Hoshea, the last king of Israel who ruled only because Assyria installed him in that position? What Israel sowed it was now reaping. *And judgment sprouts like poisonous weeds in the furrows of the field,* 10:4.

In Hebrew *Bethel* meant "house of God." In Hosea 10:5, the name Bethel is changed to *Beth-aven,* which means "house of vanity." The center of their worship was going to be vacated and there was nothing the "calf-god" could do to stop the march of the enemy. In fact, the golden calf would be carried off to Assyria and paid as tribute to the king (*King Jareb*). All the worship they offered to the calf profited them nothing. They would be reduced to shame. A day was coming when the king and his court would be destroyed and the high places around Bethel (Aven) would be destroyed. Where once men had paraded around singing praises to their idols, *thorns and thistles* would grow up on their altars. The wording in the last part of 10:8 is extremely sad. As the people suffered greatly, they would cry out for a quick death rather than continue to experience the life of torture they endured. This same language is used by Isaiah in Isaiah 2:19 in describing the desire of the inhabitants of Judah as they are destroyed by the Babylonians. In Luke 23:30, Jesus also described the reaction of those dealing with the destruction of Jerusalem in this way. Finally, in Revelation 6:14-16, the punishment of those who persecuted saints in the first few centuries after Jesus' death is described in this way.

Israel had a long history of sin

The days of Gibeah are a reminder of the incident in Judges where a concubine of a Levite was brutally raped, Judges 19. Hosea has already refreshed the memories of his audience with a mentioning of the tragic event in Hosea 9:9. This generation (that of Hosea's day) was just as guilty as those who sinned in Judges. They were going to be severely chastised by the Assyrians. What is the *double guilt* Hosea mentions in 10:10? Some feel it is in reference to their stubbornness in having man-made kings over them and for completely rejecting God by turning to worship man-made objects.[1] In 10:11, Hosea likens Israel to a young heifer who *loves to thresh*. While this metaphor might go missed by American audiences who are for the most part separated from agrarian societies, it rang home to the people of Hosea's day. Young heifers that were trained to thresh the grain were treated with kindness and would have enjoyed their work because of the obvious benefit: they got to eat as much as they wanted. The role Israel was used to playing was about to be abruptly changed. God was going to harness them (both Judah and Israel) and subject them to the work of slaves as punishment for their ungodliness.

A call to repentance

Going from here to the end of the chapter, Hosea calls on his people to repent. They did not have to suffer this terrible fate if they would just turn to God. They were called to *Sow with a view to righteousness* and *reap in accordance with kindness,* 10:12. If they would turn to the Lord quickly, He would come to *rain righteousness on you [them]*, 10:12. This was a people who needed to repent with the quickest urgency. But this was a people who had bought into the lies they told themselves. They were living in an alternate reality. They trusted in themselves, their military, their fortresses, and their alliances. This was a people who would not listen to the calls to turn back to God.

Beth-arbel was located west of the Sea of Galilee. *Shalman* was probably a shortened form of Shalmaneser,[2] and could be referring to an invasion by Shalmaneser IV in 773 B.C. Or the Shalmaneser could be referring to Shalmaneser V who was reigning at the fall of Samaria in 722 B.C. Whenever this battle took place, it was one that contained incredible human cruelty; *mothers were dashed in pieces with their children,* 10:14. This was going to happen to the Israelites because of their great wickedness.

God loved Israel, but they continually showed their ingratitude

Again, we get the idea of God's extreme hurt over Israel's conduct. God loved Israel. He loved them so much He took them out of bondage in Egypt to their own land where He could raise and nurture them. *Yet it is I who taught Ephraim to walk, I took them in My arms; But they did not know that I healed them. I led them with cords of a man, with the bonds of love… I bent down and fed them,* 11:3-4. God was constantly moved with love, care, and compassion for them. As we read these verses, it is not hard to be reminded of the parent-child relationship. Parents often do so much for their children—more than the children realize. This was the case with God and Israel. God shows His dismay over all of this in verse two: *The more they called them, the more they went from them; They kept sacrificing to the Baals And burning incense to idols.*

While the first part of 11:5 may appear to contradict other references to Egypt and slavery, we know that the earlier references were metaphors. As the people were slaves in Egypt before God rescued them, so they would be again—but not in Egypt. This time Assyria would be their master because they refused to return to God. Here are a people who were *bent on turning from* [God], 11:7. They would be destroyed and consumed by their enemies.

Chapter eleven not only opens with God's emotion being poured out, but it closes with it as well. Because of the punishment God was bringing upon them, His *heart is* [*was*] *turned over within Me, All My compassions are kindled,* 11:8. The idea of reducing Israel to nothing was heart-wrenching for God. God did not delight in what He was about to do. Admah and Zeboiim were cities in the area around Sodom and Gomorrah which were destroyed when God rained down judgment in Genesis 19. See also Deuteronomy 29:23 which references these cities. In fact, Deuteronomy 29:24-26 fits in quite well with Hosea's writing since what was prophesied so many centuries before was about to take place.

God was not going to annihilate His people. While justice needed to be poured out, God would, through His mercy and grace, allow a remnant to continue living to carry on the promises made to Abraham and David. After the period of chastisement, God's people would follow Him. As they were released from slavery, they would return to live with Him.

Lessons for Today

The high costs associated with sin

Israel had always counted on their place with God and His constant protection from enemies. But because of their gross sin and immorality, they would pay the ultimate price. God would turn His back on them as the Assyrians march in destroying their culture, cities, and nation. They paid the highest cost for the pleasure and status of worshipping idols. Let us always remember that sin always pays us back in ways we never expected or could have imagined at the time of the temptation.

We must always remember the source of our blessings

They had achieved much for themselves—a good economy, a place on the world stage, a strong military, and bountiful crops. All of this would be stripped away. In fact, everything that they would associate with a national identity would be destroyed by the Assyrians. The country forgot God. What about us? How strong is our consciousness of God and the extent of His blessings upon us?

Sin can place us in an alternate reality

The most dangerous lie is the lie we tell ourselves. Israel deluded itself into thinking that everything was O.K. and that there was no cause for alarm. Even if the enemy did attack, surely their fortresses would hold. Surely their armies would fight back the enemy. Surely those Assyrians didn't really mean to destroy them. This alternate world of reality would soon come crashing down upon them. How many souls are deluded today and headed down the path away from God—all while telling themselves everything is O.K.

God does not enjoy punishing mankind

Chapter eleven is one of the most moving passages in all the Old Testament. Here we see a side of God that should impress us with the extent of His grace, mercy, and love. God is not some distant, aloof being who does not feel a connection to His creation. He felt a genuine hurt and His heart was moved at the thought of allowing them to be punished. In the New Testament we are told that God does not wish that anyone be lost, but He desires all men come to repentance, 2 Peter 3:9.

For discussion

1. Would Israel literally return to Egypt as part of its punishment from God? If not, what does the wording in 9:3 mean?

2. As Hosea wrote the words of his prophecy, had the judgment of God already begun to take place? See 9:6-7.

3. In what way does what we worship influence us? See 9:10.

4. Consult a study Bible and note some of the great events that took place at Gilgal. What had become of Gilgal in the days of Hosea?

5. In Hebrew Bethel meant: "_____ _____ _____" Beth-aven meant: "_____ _____ _____" Describe the irony in the usage of Beth-aven in describing the central place of worship for the northern kingdom.

6. What do the days of Gibeah refer to?

7. Israel is called on to repent in 10:12. Why is the sense of urgency so great in these verses?

8. Describe the cruelty that took place at Beth-arbel.

9. Describe God's feelings when considering how He was going to chastise Israel. Why is it important to see this side of God?

10. Where were Admah and Zeboiim?

11. Would God destroy His people?

Chapter Endnotes

1   Both Hailey and Smith take this point of view. Hubbard points out that this is similar to Jeremiah's "two-sins" (2:13).

2   Smith, James E. *The Minor Prophets.* p. 263.

Ephraim's Great Sin

Introduction

As we move into the last section of Hosea, the attention returns to the sins of Ephraim. This tribe (which represented the northern tribes as a whole) pursued *the east wind continually.* Feeding on the wind and pursing the east wind were symbolic language describing actions that were made in vain. An east wind was often associated with destruction. It was never good. This was a nation that was going to be destroyed because of its lies and violence. No thought was given to God, and as Assyria approached, they made alliances with them. The covenant with Assyria was made during the reign of Menahem when he agreed to pay tribute to Tiglath-pileser. As the alliance with Assyria faded, Israel looked to Egypt for assistance. To sweeten the deal, they sent oil to Egypt during the reign of Hoshea, 2 Kings 17:4; Hosea 12:1. Not only did God have a case against the northern ten tribes, but He also had *a dispute with Judah,* 12.2. Although Judah would be in existence for around another one hundred forty years, they too would pay for their rebelliousness.

Beginning at the end of verse two, God reminds His people of Jacob. Jacob was the ancestor of both Israel and Judah, and he would be well known to them. Hosea recalls that Jacob took hold of his brother Esau by the heel in the womb. Later Jacob would wrestle with an angel and prevail. Jacob sought God and found Him. Jacob's experience at Bethel was spiritual. It moved him closer to God, and it is where he began a real, meaningful relationship with God. It is at Bethel where Jacob was given the name "Israel." The point of reminding the people of Jacob is that if they would approach God in prayer, they could experience the same blessings Jacob enjoyed. They needed to look to God. *Therefore, return to your God, observe kindness and justice, and wait for your God continually,* 12:6. If the people would just return, God would relent from His certain destruction and punishment on the nation. Even to the last possible moment, God holds out for the repentance of those He loves.

But Ephraim's (Israel's) heart was far away from returning to God. They enjoyed oppressing others. False standards of measurement (12:7) and dishonest business practices had become the norm. Because of these practices, they had become rich. Amid all the wealth they found they forgot God. He had enabled them to obtain the wealth, Deuteronomy 8:17-18. They were proud of the way they had obtained their wealth: through fraud and deceit. This had become "business as usual." No wrong was seen in it whatsoever. What does this say about the level of morality in their society? God says they would be abased. They would be made to *live in tents again*, 12:9. God had continually blessed them with physical necessities. He had spoken to them through the prophets. He had nurtured them for over seven hundred years. His patience had finally reached the bitter end. The Lord was going to *leave his bloodguilt on him and bring back his reproach to him*, 12:14.

Spiritual death

As we move into chapter thirteen, we see that Israel had no more spiritual life remaining. At one time Ephraim was a powerful tribe, wielding much influence upon the other eleven tribes. But Ephraim had also fully embraced the worship of Baal, and because of that, he died spiritually. They multiplied their sins upon themselves by the great efforts they exerted to construct idols from silver. Special craftsmen were employed to set up these idols and many hours of labor were expended. For what? Did these idols have power? Could they bless the people? Could they protect Israel from the enemy? These idols which were constructed by men would *be like the morning cloud and like the dew which soon disappears, like chaff which is blown away from the threshing floor And like smoke from a chimney*, 13:3. The idols would be powerless against the one, true God. Just as dew evaporates in the morning sun, so would the people as they succumbed to the great enemy who would overtake their land.

There are more touching words in verses four and five. Here God reminds His people of the special relationship He had with them since taking them from the land of Egypt so many generations before. The relationship He had with them was personal in nature. He reminds them of the covenant they made with Him, promising not to have any other god besides God. *For there is no savior besides Me*, 13:4. God had sustained them through the wilderness. He had given them food and water in a land of drought. After bringing them in the land, they were able to settle down. Their dependence on and need for God lessened, and they soon became puffed with pride and forgot God. Because of this, God, the one who had been their shepherd, would now be as a lion and leopard to them, lying in wait by the wayside. He would encounter them by surprise. The people would be devoured, that is, destroyed.

The kings the people raised up and trusted were now powerless against the enemy. As we move through Hosea's ministry, this fact becomes more and more evident as the Assyrians insert puppet regimes before completely taking over the nation. The kings could not turn the tide against the enemy. Verse eleven is especially interesting and goes a long way in describing God's feelings about having kings over the nation. God gave them the kings they wanted but did not happily do so. And their sins were not forgotten. In fact, all the kings of the Northern Kingdom were evil and rebellious. Their deeds would be repaid with the judgment of God. Verse thirteen is especially descriptive of the problems facing the nation. Israel was as a woman who was having difficulty in childbirth. This was a common figure of speech in Old Testament literature. Both the mother and child were in danger. Ephraim was in danger of grave punishment.

Complete destruction

Israel would be annihilated. *Compassion will be hidden from My sight,* 13:14. God had finally reached a point where His compassion had run out. The reference to the east wind is made again, and more language of destruction is listed throughout verses fifteen and sixteen. Everything that was precious to the nation would be plundered, her soldiers would be taken out and their children and women would die violent deaths. It is an unpleasant scene as chapter thirteen concludes.

Hope for the future

Hosea calls for the nation to repent. They needed to return to the Lord. They had stumbled because of their great iniquity. If they would follow through and work deeds of repentance, God would forgive them. But this had to be genuine repentance. Dependence upon God was necessary. They would need to completely reject their idols. In their immediate future, if they repented, God would *heal their apostasy and love them freely* because God's *anger has turned away from them.* In this was a sense of urgency. If they were to experience these promises, repentance had to come now! God promises to replenish their physical needs, 14:5-7.

God reminds His people once more of the futility of idols. God was the one who looked out for them. He blessed them with their physical necessities, not Baal. Those who were wise would understand this. They would know that *the ways of the Lord are right and the righteous will walk in them,* 14:9. Those who rejected this wisdom would stumble.

For discussion

1. What did it mean to feed on the wind and pursue an east wind?

2. What does it say about the character of God in holding out for their repentance to the last possible moment? Are there any applications for our generation?

3. Describe the business practices of Israel during the days of Hosea.

4. How does Hosea describe the futility of worshiping idols? Did they have any real and lasting power?

5. What kind of relationship had God desired to have with Israel?

6. Once Israel received the Promised Land and became prosperous, they forgot God. They looked to their blessings and refused to give glory to God. Describe how we can fall into the same trap today.

7. How significant is 13:14? Is God's compassion unending? Why is this important for us to know?

8. If Israel was going to repent, how long did they have to do it? What would happen if they genuinely repented?

9. What if they rejected the wisdom offered in the book of Hosea?

Endnotes

1   Luckenbill, "Ancient Records of Assyria and Babylonia," pp. 443, 447. Quoted by James E. Smith, *The Minor Prophets* (Joplin, MO: College Press, 1994), p. 102.

2   Hailey, Homer E., *A Commentary on the Minor Prophets* (Louisville, KY: Religious Supply, 1993), p. 65.

3   *Coffman's Bible Commentary,* Copyright © 1971–1993 by ACU Press, Abilene Christian University.

4   Hailey, Homer E. *A Commentary on the Minor Prophets* (Louisville, KY: Religious Supply, 1993), p. 80.

5   Smith, James E., *The Minor Prophets.,* p. 122.